Praise for *Seeds of Potentiality*

"This beautiful body of work supports one's personal journey of self-discovery, inner healing, and growth. Melissa has an innate sense of self, and she uses this gift to guide us through our own personal development. She not only leads us down the path of self-care, she enlightens the readers on how important and significant we are to ourselves, those around us, and the planet."

David Villareal, PharmD and
Board-Certified Clinical Musician
www.thetherapeuticguitarist.com

"Melissa Thompson shares her personal journey into deeper connection to her authentic self. She inspires readers to discover their own North Star as a guide to what has heart and meaning. Thompson instructs how to plant and cultivate seeds of joy, creativity, and gratitude though simple steps she has woven into her busy life as mother, wife, and professional. This book will especially support young women and mothers who want to nurture their lives, those they love and Mother Earth."

Elizabeth Murray
Author, Artist, Teacher
www.elizabethmurray.com

"This book is a soft, powerful guide for inner journeys of any kind. It's a rare gem and a truly unique spiritual handbook. You will find a wealth of beautiful meditations, suggested practices, inspiring stories of the author's own inner visions and quests, practical wisdom, and truly fresh insights. Melissa seamlessly blends all these elements with a magical quality. *Seeds of Potentiality* is an invitation to remember your own, one-of-a-kind life force – perfect now and perfect in all of its ever-unfolding potential!"

Christina Brittain, MFA
Creator of *The Lighten Your Vibe* and *The Comfort* coloring books
www.christinabrittain.com

"Melissa weaves her science mind and her rich spiritual journey into vivid metaphors that show us how to live in alignment with ourselves and the natural world."

Jennifer Allen, MS, LMFT-ATR-BC
Author of *Bone Knowing: A True Story of Coming to Life in the Face of Impending Loss.*
www.boneknowing.com

"*Seeds of Potentiality* is a read that will leave you feeling nourished and inspired. Through her insightful attention to detail, Melissa beautifully invites the reader into deeper self-reflection and awareness, reminding us of the elements that are required for life to thrive. Through cultivating the 'soil of our soul' we can assure that the seeds of our dreams will have the greatest potential to flourish. Melissa lovingly encourages us to awaken our 'inner scientist' by becoming ever more curious about our inner terrain, life circumstances, and emotional experiences. As you read this book you will find yourself looking through a microscope at your own life, 'digging deeper' and becoming the 'creative gardener' that you must be to manifest your hearts desires. Melissa beautifully weaves together vignettes from her personal life experiences to illustrate healing connections that have made profound differences in her life, while also offering many resources as she shares the wisdom and teachings of others that have made the biggest impacts in her life."

Liscia DiGiacamo, HHP, Somatic Practitioner
www.dancinghandsbodywork.com

"Weaving together science, psychology, and memoir, Melissa Thompson seeds the psyche of the reader, creating a fertile ground from which new and surprising sprouts can emerge."

Cristin DeVine, LMFT, MEd and Peter Fonken, MS
www.counselingcarmel.com

"*Seeds of Potentiality* is a beautifully written map 'home'. This book will guide you along your own personal journey to discover who you are and what's important to you. The result is an authentic, deeply fulfilling life."

Amy Johnson, PhD
Author of *The Little Book of Big Change: The No-Willpower Approach to Breaking Any Habit* and *Just a Thought: A No-Willpower Approach to End Self-Doubt and Make Peace with Your Mind*
www.dramyjohnson.com

Seeds of Potentiality

A Guide to the Life Cycle of Personal Growth

MELISSA THOMPSON

The author would like to thank the following authors for their permission to reprint:
Sean Scheuering, "Melodies" from The Art and Heart of Drum Circles, copyright © 2003 by Christine Stevens. Reprinted with permission from Christine Stevens.
Christina Brittain, "Point of Joy" from The Lighten Your Vibe Coloring Book, copyright © 2016 by Christina Brittain. Reprinted with permission from Christina Brittain.
Rachel Parent, "Thoughts on Seeds" from www.seewhatgrows.org, copyright © January 2017. Reprinted with permission from Rachel Parent.

First Printing, 2021

ISBN-13: 978-1-956503-49-4 print edition
ISBN-13: 978-1-956503-50-0 ebook edition

DreamSculpt Books and Media
An imprint of:

Waterside Productions
Waterside Productions
2055 Oxford Ave
Cardiff, CA 92007
www.waterside.com

Dedication

This book is for my son, Declan, and for the spirit of generations to come.

Declan's curiosity, innocence, and zest for life inspire me beyond my wildest imagination. He has opened doors in my mind and my heart that I didn't even know existed.

I hope that his beautiful soul sprouts and flowers the most amazing garden cultivated by his inquisitive spirit's joy, love, and bliss.

Table of Contents

The Day Hike: An Introduction

The early morning fog created a quiet heaviness that hung low on the branches of the trees as I set out on my adventure. The well-worn split rail fence marked the trailhead. I could smell the damp moisture in the air. It was a familiar path that I had hiked several times with friends and family members. Yet, as I embarked upon the trail, I felt drawn to take a direction I had never explored before. A fallen tree and a bowed branch marked the portal into my alternative hike that would pour forth metaphors and images that would stay with me for years. This excursion was my day hike, a day dedicated to exploring and wandering with no expectations.

After hiking partway up the trail, the first place I rested was beside a small pool of dark and mysterious water. It was an ephemeral pool created by recent rains and reflected roots emerging from the eroded soil. I found a small rock to perch upon and pulled out my notebook. As I sketched and jotted down my reflections, I realized that this pool was a place of letting go—the beginning of the transition I would experience on my vision fast. I heard the call to unpack the burdens I was facing in my life. This day, this hike, was a time to remove myself from my normal daily activities and look within. It was a door to the time I would soon spend in the wilderness and the beginning of a greater connection to myself. Imagine the reflective nature of water. It's cool and calm. Sometimes when we peer into the water and see our reflection, we see things from a new perspective.

As I continued my hike, I came to a lush fern grotto. The beauty here was in stark contrast to the eroded and barren landscape surrounding the pool of water. I felt a rush of joy and connection, along with a sense of rebirth. Little did I know that these metaphors and images I was experiencing along the trail were preparing me for my expedition into the wilderness.

The day hike was an initiation for my upcoming vision fast. My purpose for participating in this adventure was to seek a deeper connection with myself and, ultimately, my community. The day hike was a preparatory exercise meant to expose me to the concept of wandering freely by myself and using the time for reflection and introspection. In addition, it was a twelve-hour fast, which allowed me to connect with nature without the distractions of preparing or breaking for food.

Wilderness rites of passage such as vision fasts are a Native American tradition that is practiced in other indigenous cultures around the world. It's a ritual that marks a time of transition or rebirth. It's a time to allow nature to reflect the beauty of our inherent state. I am using the term vision fast here to describe my personal experience of a venture I embarked upon to look more deeply into my life. The vision is the insight that comes from removing oneself from the distractions of modern life. This illumination may be the appearance of a spirit guide, a renewed awareness of the beauty of life, or a deeper connection to a spiritual tradition. The pancultural aspect of the vision fast is a time for quiet contemplation—a fast from the comforts and distractions of daily life.

Throughout this book, you will learn about the journey of seeds. They are the seeds of potentiality, and they live in you. They are simply waiting to arrive in your consciousness. And when they arrive, you can plant them, tend to them, and help them grow. Your time with this book is your opportunity to discover your seeds of potentiality and help them flourish by creating a nourishing garden of life. Allow the concepts you encounter to act as a refreshing pool of water where you may find insights and clarity. Drink from the wellspring and quench your desire for contentment.

Cultivate an openness to explore. As you read about experiences and insights from my life journey, approach them as a curious day hiker out to see what's new on the trail. Some ideas may inspire you, and others may not resonate. The intention is not for you to walk away with a prescription for how to live your life. Instead, I am offering a trail mix of ideas and opportunities that may help you on your journey. The nourishment provided by the tasty morsels is an understanding that personal growth is a life cycle, a process that continues to refine and define how we live out our days. I'm not going to offer a set of numbered steps to achieve a goal. Because as much as we would like growth and change to be linear, we often find that we may need to repeat some steps, or create new actions, to stay consistent with the outcome of our initial efforts. Repetition of processes helps them become ingrained in who we are. And it's okay if we fail the first time we try something new. There is an immense capacity to learn from our setbacks and perceived failures. We are always learning, and I find that when I revisit something repeatedly, it starts to impact my life.

This life cycle of personal growth is something that started as a personal mantra over a decade ago. When I felt stuck or needed motivation again, I would say to myself, "Create, cultivate, celebrate." These words have become ingrained in my heart and mind; they are the mantra that pulls me into the present. These words are an anchor, a grounding tool, to help me get more deeply rooted in the reality unfolding right before me. Whether struggling with a decision about my life path or realizing I was in a whirlwind of thought, I recognized that I had the power to create the next moment. I saw the opportunity to cultivate life.

Over the years, this mindset has brought me home to myself with greater ease and acceptance than other remedies I have tried. To return to my mantra of "create, cultivate, celebrate" feels accessible and straightforward. I feel light and alive when I connect with the innate creativity of being human. And when I recognize that I can cultivate what is happening in my life, I accept my responsibility for how I'm living. Lastly, I celebrate both the successes and the setbacks. When I am living fully, I am learning from the wins as well as the failures.

A dear friend and I spoke recently about how it's time to leave the wounding mythology behind and emerge into a time of potential. What does this mean to make this shift? This shift is a call to action to bring our gifts—those seeds of potentiality—into the world. They no longer need to hide in the hurt and despair of past patterns or hide in the shadows of our upbringing. They simply need to be planted, cultivated, and then celebrated as they come to life.

The genesis of this cycle lies within the seeds of potentiality. These seeds are the thoughts, ideas, concepts, and sparks of joy that pull us toward a greater vision of what life would look like if we planted one and cultivated its growth. Take contentment, for example. When we plant the intention of wanting to live a more content life, we have taken the first step of inviting this perspective into how we are living. Once planted, we choose to cultivate its potential to grow into a rich and fulfilling life. Cultivating is connecting with what the seed needs in order to grow and become established. We move away from worry and concern over where life is heading, and we start living more in the present moment. We learn techniques that support this mindful way of living. Thus, we begin to shift and change. We are not changing the essence of who we are, but rather the connection to our true nature is deepening as we release the external world of what-ifs and should-have-beens.

When I crested the top of the rocky terrain during my day hike, there was a bench where I was able to sit and take in the vistas.

While you explore the landscape of your soul, make sure you take moments to pause so you can appreciate the trails you have traveled and look out to the opportunities ahead. When you stop and reflect on the path of life, you will come across places to plant the seeds of potentiality that life has given you.

That day when I descended the trail back to my starting point, I kept noticing seeds, and I had an epiphany about how seeds travel. I realized that some are hitchhikers, some take flight, and some go with the flow. The hitchhikers latch on to things—people's clothes, animal fur, and other fabrics of life—that move them toward their destination. Others have wings and soar. And a few find the flow of rivers and streams that carry them to their place of expansion. The seeds hold pure potential. They intend to grow. But first, they need to find an area to be planted. And thus, the journey begins.

Unveil life's beauty. It's ready to be witnessed.

There is a tree that stands out among the others.
She is a tree that withstands time. The elements have weathered her bark, and though aspects of her appearance may appear frail, her balanced strength is preserved by the sprawling roots that run over and under the rocks of the terrain in which she stands.
She is a master of witnessing change without judgment. With each year, she adds a ring of remembrance and grows in her wisdom.
As a home to many creatures, she is a refuge providing comfort to those who come to her. Within her shelter, there is a community of creatures connecting and living in harmony.
She invites you to listen to her stories about seeds and how their potential pushes through their shell to become the thing they are destined to be.

Chapter 1

THE GRANDMOTHER TREE

My body was supported by the sturdy trunk of an established tree whose roots drove deep into the earth and intertwined with the terrain of the hillside. This was the "grandmother tree" I encountered on my vision fast. The intricacies of her root system provided the perfect resting spot. I settled into her exposed roots, enjoying the view of a delightful babbling brook and the sunlit clearing beyond. Her warmth held me in the uncertainty of this foreign experience. She was a strong tree and a witness to the stories of the land. Now she was witnessing my story. She was the reason I selected this spot for my time in the woods. Safe and secure in her presence, I reflected on what brought me to this landscape. It was an ideal location for quiet reflections and to initiate a deeper internal rooting—a time to cultivate the soil of my soul.

The road to reach the grandmother tree was a small two-lane highway that meandered through an idyllic countryside town. The winding road carved out our path into the wilderness to the starting point for the venture. As we left the cities and neighborhoods behind, the dwellings became more sparse, and the route dwindled into a dusty dirt road, taking us deeper into the forest. The terrain shifted from familiar to unknown. Finally we reached a small pullout where just a handful of cars could park. My fellow travelers and I unloaded the cars and put on our packs. We headed into the wilderness to explore both internal and external landscapes, refrain from eating, and abstain from worldly comforts. Our small group abandoned the familiar as we set off into the woods for an unforgettable experience.

The untouched beauty of the land was awe-inspiring. There was not a structure in sight. The call of a hawk overhead rang out as we noticed the occasional fellow hiker on the trail. The initial trail into the wilderness reminded me of other hikes and explorations I enjoyed over the years. From family hikes in the foothills of Santa Barbara to epic day hikes along the Big Sur coastline, my life was filled with sweet memories of taking in the joy of fresh air and the natural beauty encountered in the outdoors. As we traversed down to the valley floor, the terrain shifted from the vistas of the peaks and valleys at the higher altitude to a denser forest.

We were a small group of four participants and two guides. As I thought back to the previous day of preparations, I realized that the three other participants were individuals I had just met the day before. Our initial meeting was in the teepee on the property owned by the guides for our vision fast. The opening ceremony was a communal circle around a sacred drum where the group shared stories of how and why we decided to participate in this pilgrimage. The drum held a deep significance for the guides as the initial owner was a dear mentor who had just passed in a tragic accident. It was an honor to sit before this instrument and feel the resonance deep in our souls.

Back on the trail, moving into deeper woods, we became aware of the physical wilderness, and at the same time, the wilds of the inner self. What will we find while traveling the terrain of our thoughts and feelings? Where would my imagination go as the exploration of the unknown unfolded? The chaos of my busy life and the tensions of my mind began to relax and unravel. My job, my master's program, my relationships, even my to-do lists were all left behind. Instead, all my attention shifted to this retreat in the backcountry of the soul.

My preparation for the trip included shedding my morning coffee habit, training for the physical trek, and reflecting on what connections I wanted to cultivate deep within. Now, as we headed out to seek our visions, the pounding of feet on the dusty trail brought our hearts in tune with the rhythm of the drum from the prior night's gathering. Our backpacks were heavy, yet we felt energized and exuberant about the journey ahead.

Visions

I first met our guides, Cristin and Peter, while dancing my heart out one cool October night under a full moon. Their exuberance for life was evident on the dance floor. They had nurtured a gathering of self-expression that initiated a life-changing chapter in my life. Connecting with them grounded me in a community that warmed my soul and nurtured my personal growth. Cristin's ability to stay rooted and connected to the earth while spinning a vortex of energy to the spirit world speaks to her shamanistic capacity. Peter's rugged yet soulful approach to life reveals his reverence for the natural world and his desire to heed the calling to bring others into contact with the depths of their inner world.

Cristin and Peter are two people I trust deeply. Their personal and professional training qualifies them to skillfully lead groups into the wilderness and listen to the individual seeking more profound understanding, the soul's inner knowing. When inquiring about their development of our excursion in the wilderness, Cristin shared that the framework for our expedition was a fusion of 13 years of studying Soulcraft at Animas Valley Institute and many years of studying indigenous and non-indigenous models of the vision fast and initiatory rites of passage. Incorporating the teachings of Bill Plotkin, a psychologist, wilderness guide, and founder of the institute, Cristin and Peter's model of self-exploration excels in the process of leading seekers into the woods, embracing solitude, and encountering the most challenging aspect of life: ourselves.

The vision fast has been practiced for thousands of years by countless cultures—the individual at a life transition stepping into the wilderness to contemplate their true essence. In Cristin's sharing, she reflected that this rite of passge is a way to unplug from the dominant programming of the culture (and our everyday lives), which gives us the ability to listen to the deep knowing that is within and be in conversation with the more than human world. Moving beyond the human world brings us closer to what Peter would refer to as the "collective relationship with the wild world." This emotional connection with the earth and her healing potential for humans is ecopsychology for the soul. While traveling through the adventures of this book, you will be invited to trek into the life cycle of personal growth and explore the connection between your inner wilderness and the forests of the earth.

Reflecting on the major commitments and occurences in my life at the time of my fast in the wilderness, I recall that I was working part-time as a pharmacist, studying to earn my degree in counseling psychology, and connecting with the man who would become my husband. It was a period of personal transformation and growth. I was cultivating seeds planted from my experiences that began with a yoga teacher training, continued with living and studying at Esalen Institute and Mount Madonna Center, and culminated in exploring the world of expressive arts. I will share the process of encountering these seeds and the cultivation of their growth in my life. When I ventured out on this quest, the intention was to dig deeper and tend to the soil of my inner terrain. It was a time to remove myself from the busyness and demands of life so I could examine my seeds of experience for signs of growth—seeds of hope, love, and a longing for work that would allow me to serve others and help them flourish in life. I knew that I wanted to shift my career in a direction that would blend my skills and talents. The challenge was figuring out how and when I would be able to make these changes. The process was in full effect currently in my life, and this vision fast was the time to stand back and observe the unfolding.

It takes effort to create the opportunity to shed the layers of responsibility and the demands of life to the point of simply attending to our daily survival, unveiling a naked and vulnerable self. When we strip away our titles, our digital connections, and our focus on seeking answers from the world around us, we encounter the quieter essence of who we are as an individual.

Going on an intense vision fast, as I describe here, may not be physically possible for you or the right path for your journey. However, exploring your internal terrain is available to you from a quiet, contemplative spot in your home or on a trail in your community. Your adventure is the journey within to explore your inner terrain. What brings you alive, what calms your soul, and what makes your heart sing? What is hiding in the caves and caverns of your deeper realms? Sometimes we need to remove the outer distractions in order to connect within the deepest realms of ourselves. Where are you able to find a spot of peace in your day to breathe in your essence? Being in the wilderness is an ideal catalyst for this type of work. Connecting with nature may be found in your neighborhood park, your backyard garden, the balcony of your apartment, or in the warmth of a sunlit room. Close your eyes and see the wilderness that resides within.

The Journey Inside

What if you explored the complex network of neurons, pathways, and microorganisms that live within your body? This internal ecosystem fully supports your health and wellness. When we understand the connections between our physical and emotional health, this inner exploration reveals the wilderness within. It's a rich and lively place of cellular life cycles, intricate communication systems, and endless productivity. There is something magical here that you may not know: the regenerative potential of your cells. We often get tricked into thinking that we are stuck—held in old patterns, thoughts, and circumstances. Modern scientific research reveals that the cellular structures of our bodies can rework and regenerate. Most importantly, we have the power to influence their outcomes. If this internal physical regeneration is possible, then we know that our emotional renewal is also feasible.

You may think it's hard enough to shift a single behavior and introduce a new pattern into your life without worrying about all these silly little cells. But these cells are your body. As we engage with our mind and see its relationship with our body, life begins to shift. The foods we eat, the words we speak, our emotions and feelings all influence our daily state of well-being. Our state of awareness regarding our decisions influences everything that is happening every second within our bodies and is vital for our health.

Think of the cells within your digestive system. They work tirelessly for you—breaking down foods, producing the correct number of enzymes, and allowing your body to extract the nutrients it needs from the foods you have consumed. Provide loving care for this body system through making the right decisions about what to eat, and you thrive. In contrast, what happens when you flood your system with toxins? You suffer. The mental fog sets in, and the rest of your day goes downhill. Be the master gardener of your cells by supplying them with nutrients, water, and loving care.

If we think of our bodies as the garden, the tissues as the soil, and the cells as the seeds, we see the potential to positively influence our health by how we tend to our gardens. Just as our cells are seeds of potentiality, there are metaphorical seeds that we hold within ourselves that contain our hopes, dreams, and aspirations. These conceptual seeds are being planted in a physical realm—your body. We are multidimensional creatures in a tangible world. When we embrace integrating our physical, emotional, and spiritual layers, our garden grows exponentially.

Seeds

Just as a walk in the woods leads us to discover many types of plant seeds, in our journey through life, we encounter emotional and spiritual seeds that we may choose to plant (or not) in the soil bed of life. As we travel the sidewalks, trails, and paths of our neighborhoods, forests, and communities, we encounter the changing environment that influences the cultivation of these seeds. Consider the internal and external ecosystems that influence growth.

Seeds prompt us to think of plants—the genesis of a flower, a vegetable, a tree. Seeds hold potential for growth and expansion, yet we must plant them to unlock their promise. When we connect the metaphorical seeds—what we would like to see bloom in our lives—with the physical potential of our humanity, we recognize the capacity of our cells and the treasure they hold to shift our health and wellness. The cells of our body are the physical seeds that constantly fire away to power us through the day. There is an internal communication system that oversees the relationship between our external and internal environments. For example, in order to interpret and comprehend physically spoken words, a cascade of neurotransmitters are released in reaction to the words. How we receive and respond to these spoken words is influenced by our sleep patterns, our food, and the current tenor of our relationships with others.

Why is diving into the microbiology of a cell pertinent to our conversation regarding human potential? Because it's the epicenter of our aliveness. Without the actions and reactions of the molecules—the genetic material that is the essence of life—we would not be having this conversation. I am in awe of how our bodies work. Studying the inner workings of how we function motivates me. It's what drew me to become a pharmacist. Fascinated by enzyme chemistry as an undergraduate student, wanting to learn more, I was also drawn to the development of patterns for generating health and wellness. In addition to chemistry, I studied various artistic disciplines to expand my creativity and connect to nonlinear methods of problem-solving. By connecting with concepts from biology, chemistry, physics, and the arts, we expand and grow our understanding of how humans operate. When we develop our awareness of how we can live in wholeness, our innate creativity has space to express itself. Creativity is key to achieving the balance and flow that so many of us long for. In this flow of wholeness and expression, we can delight in stillness, in the power of our breath, and the ability to mindfully approach life.

Integrations

Together, let's explore the relationship between body, mind, and spirit. The physical attributes and connectivity of our cells are influenced by the thoughts that impact our brain functionality, as found in studies of the minds and brains of Buddhist monks. In Sharon Begley's book *Train Your Mind, Change Your Brain: How a New Science*

Reveals Our Extraordinary Potential to Transform Ourselves, she examines the intricate unfolding of how neuroscience explains the potential to transform and grow: "So even though existing [neuron] cells cannot make two out of one, the brain has the seeds from which to grow whole new neurons" (Begley 2007, 56). Neurogenesis is the process in which new neurons form in the brain from neural stem cells. Science originally stated that this process only occurred in embryos and during our early years. Laura Andreae is a researcher interested in neurodevelopment who explores the debate as to the potentiality of neurogenesis in the adult brain. "Over the last two decades, overwhelming evidence gradually accumulated for the capacity of new neurons to be born in the adult brain in two clearly defined locations: the subventricular zone and the dentate gyrus (DG) of the hippocampus. The hippocampus is well known to play important roles in learning and memory, and this adult DG neurogenesis has not only been implicated in memory but has led to ideas that it could be harnessed to treat neurodegenerative and neuropsychiatric disorders. However, while the story is clear in rodents, whether and to what extent adult neurogenesis occurs in humans has remained controversial" (Andreae 2018).

A critical part of this momentum in understanding how our minds and brains work has included immense research and collaboration between the mindfulness movement and neuroscience. By building upon his background in healthcare and leveraging his passion for Ayurveda, Deepak Chopra shows how thought leaders can integrate science and meditation. Another example is Mindfulness-Based Stress Reduction (MBSR), a method developed by Jon Kabat-Zinn that blends the tools of mindfulness with the well-established therapeutic approach of cognitive-based therapy. The outcomes of the studies supporting these therapeutic approaches reveal an appreciation for the sense of peace that paying attention can bring. At Harvard Medical School, there is a group named the Mindfulness Research Collaboration, which includes physicians, neuroscientists, mathematicians, ethicists, and others who are dedicated to digging deep and understanding the science behind mindfulness. These researchers and others continue to extensively study the physical road maps of our bodily systems to understand this interweaving of the physical, emotional, and spiritual layers in our lives.

In addition to physical maps, we also have emotional maps in our bodies—paths worn into our psyche as emotional imprints of our life experiences, paths that shape who we are. When we explore these stories of our past, we connect with our roots and understand more about our ways of being in the world. Habits, beliefs, and behaviors all rise from our emotional and mental maps. Emotions are a vital aspect of our daily lives, and when we explore the genesis of the feelings that sprout up as we face challenges or celebrate successes, we understand ourselves a little more. Life makes more sense.

For many of us, the seeds of potentiality we seek to nurture are embedded in our mental state. From finding joy and contentment to satisfying the desires of our hearts, we yearn to fulfill our emotional longings. My initial concepts for this book consisted of chapters focused on creating, cultivating, and celebrating these states of being. My journey taught me that this emotional realm is held in the spans between the physical and spiritual. The mind rests within the body and seeks to connect with the spirit. Therefore, creating, cultivating, and celebrating requires a connection to body, mind, and spirit.

As a graduate student in counseling psychology, I encountered various approaches to exploring the internal emotional landscape. The biological, psychodynamic, behavioral, cognitive, and humanistic perspectives were all present in my education. I found myself wanting to weave aspects of each discipline into my paradigm. Part of the beauty of the graduate program I attended was the opportunity to organically experience and explore the various modes of healing we were didactically encountering. Experiential role-playing, where we revealed the deeper, more private layers of our souls to our peers, expanded our awareness of the interpersonal interchange in therapeutic relationships. Our transformation was not only academic but a process of transpersonal healing.

I distinctly remember standing in my white aikido outfit in the school dojo and experiencing the visceral tightening as my opponent confronted me. However, the lessons demonstrated that I could move gracefully through the space with the individual I was standing face-to-face with by finding flow and centering myself. This experience translates to our relationships, both personal and professional, outside the dojo. Integrating these teachings into our interpersonal conversations, they become dynamic, more profound, and graceful.

When we explore the connection beyond our physical body and our emotional state, we expand into the larger realm of the transpersonal. There are many paths to connect us with spirit. For me, this path is about creativity and nature. I recognize something as part of my spiritual path when I come alive in its presence—sunrise opens my heart every morning, bird song from beyond my window fills me with delight. Drawing or painting raises the vibration of my body, and I feel connected with myself and the creative process. Both creativity and nature are found in the spiritual traditions of the world. Contemplate this question: How do **you** connect with the spiritual realm?

Over the years, I have practiced and studied various spiritual traditions. Spirit reveals itself to me when time slows and the physical framework of life pulls apart, displaying the smaller components of its fabric. You can imagine this revelation. Take something you know in the physical realm—this book, for instance. Watch the book unfold as you study each page, then each word, then each letter as it separates into individual parts. The book comes to life because the letters make up words, the words form sentences, the sentences tell you a story, and the story becomes a book.

In the same way, your physical body is made of components, and those components become you. And if we look a little deeper, we see that emotional and spiritual webs of existence are similar. They can be broken down into beliefs, thoughts, dreams, and hopes. And how these emotional and spiritual webs are imprinted onto the physical framework of our existence influences how we portray ourselves to the world.

Your physical, emotional, and spiritual frameworks can change and adapt as you journey through life. Within those frameworks, the cells, the thoughts, and the blessings are the seeds of potentiality that live within you. We have not been cast out of the garden. We are **in** the garden of our lives, where we are learning that there is no inside or outside. We are all one. The polarities dissolve, and our essence is revitalized as we connect with our purpose. Everyone is a living piece of the whole, a cell in the organism of humanity.

Weaving neuroscience, mindfulness, and creative expression generates a grounded and organic process—a life cycle of personal growth—that will support and encourage you on your life journey. Next, let's explore that life cycle and begin connecting with the regenerative energy it brings to our potential.

Life cycles

The grandmother tree I met during my time in the wilderness started as a seed. She then burst into life by breaking through the shell of her covering and creating a sprout, which grew mightily. She cultivated her existence as a stable and robust tree, recording life experiences in the rings of her trunk. Her wisdom deepened, life weathered her bark, and her roots reached over and under the terrain. This life cycle of potential-holding seed to newly formed sprout to maturing, magnificent tree will continue as new seeds emerge from her and find their times and places to be planted and come to life.

How do we navigate these life cycles in our physical, emotional, and spiritual lives? Often the wisdom of a "grandmother tree" can provide guidance. The grandmother tree is a metaphor for the person or entity supporting and encouraging us in our life journeys. Some of us may have an auntie, brother, mentor, or someone who connects us to the rhythms and knowing of life. When you find a "tree" that connects you to life, that is a grandmother tree. The lessons and guidance you learn from these wise people point you to the wisdom of nature that resides, grows, and expands from within you.

How do you know what **you** can create, manifest, or bring forth in this life? Many of us assume that specific skills and capacities limit us. What if you discover you have more potential than you realized? My perspective on creativity is through the lens of possibility. To create is to bring forth something that was not previously present—from a place of potential into the reality of being. Take something we all experience during the day, eating a meal, for example. The ingredients existed before you or the person who prepared the meal combined them into the soup, salad, or sandwich you enjoyed for lunch. Those ingredients held the potential to become your meal. The chef combined them to create something new. This food is what you enjoy by engaging your senses and experiencing the creation. Creating a meal may seem simple, yet it's a fantastic example of how potential can manifest new substance for your life.

Seeds are living inside of you that are ready to create. Create new ways of being in the world, new relationships, new business entities, new... you name it! **You** can create. Everyone can. Why? Because human potential is innate. You embody potential beyond what you ever imagined. Envision shifting your perspective in a way that introduces more peace and contentment into your daily life. Consider the level of enjoyment from generating more energy to connect with your family and friends. What would it look like to step into a garden of life that hummed and buzzed with beauty and relationship?

Life teems with potential. Potential is found in the kinetics of physics, the elements of chemistry, and the cells of biology. These scientific disciplines are part of your everyday life—from the steam rising from that morning cup of coffee to the hinges swinging the doors open in your home to the movement of your body.

From the unfurling of a flower bud into full bloom to the amazing process of two single cells merging to become a human being—potential abounds. How do these seeds of potential come to life? Through their life cycles. In this paradigm of personal growth, the life cycle begins with seeds of potentiality activated by our creativity, nurtured by our cultivation, and harvested in our celebration.

The life cycle of personal growth starts with the seeds of potentiality. It may be simply a spark of joy about an idea or an inkling that something could be different in how you perceive a situation. Once that seed is recognized, it can create an entire ecosystem in your life. For example, the joy I felt when thinking about writing a book flickered for almost ten years. When I finally heeded the call and began to write this book, I entered the next phase: creation.

Creation is taking that spark or inkling and acting upon it—responding to the call. Joseph Campbell teaches us of heeding the call in *The Hero with a Thousand Faces* and *The Power of Myth.* "The usual hero adventure begins with someone from whom something has been taken, or who feels there is something lacking in the normal experience available or permitted to the members of society. The person then takes off on a series of adventures beyond the ordinary, either to recover what has been lost or to discover some life-giving elixir. It's usually a cycle, a coming and a returning" (Campbell 1991, 152). We all have the potential to be heroes—heroes in our own lives and the lives of those around us. I was first introduced to the work of Joseph Campbell in high school, and reading *The Hero with a Thousand Faces* planted seeds, seeds that would return in years to come. In *The Power of Myth,* Campbell talks about the power of this monomyth and its ability to shape new beginings, new ways of living. "In order to found something new, one has to leave the old and go in quest of the seed idea, a germinal idea that will have the potentiality of bringing forth that new thing" (Campbell 1991, 167).

One of the ways this story returned to me, and the seed sprouted in my adult life, was through the transformative expressive arts experience I had with my teacher, Jane Goldberg. Jane's good-natured spirit and lively expression brought the material to life. Her smile radiated assurance that the fear of singing in front of others or sharing a deep feeling that arose from an image would be met with warmth. Through my training with her, the evolution of the hero's journey returned to my life. This time it was not simply a cognitive exploration of Campbell's words but a lived experience as I acted out my rendition of the hero's cycle. In this exploration of the timeless monomyth of departure, initiation, and return, we considered the aspects of the various phases in our own lives. The participants shared the tensions of conflict, uncertainty, and fear through improvisational interplay. By using costumes, movement, tonality, and interpersonal dialogue, our stories of wounding began to heal.

Who are the guardians at the threshold between the known and the unknown? What challenges do we face, and who are our helpers along the journey? At the crux of our initiation, what is revealed? And in the process of our return, what does our transformation look like? These are all amazing aspects of our journey as the hero of our lives. Reflect, explore, and evaluate how life calls us into the unknown to change us. Once changed, we return to the known with the gift of perspective we received on our adventure.

This book explores the seeds of potentiality that live within **you**. These seeds create connections and networks in the fabric of your being that will help you develop resilience, find contentment, and sing with joy. I believe that **all of us are creative**. Therefore, I am taking the concept of creativity beyond the paintbrush, the song, and the poem and extending it to anything you create.

What would you like to create? Are you looking for more time with your family? How about space to plant a garden? Is it love, health, wealth, or positivity? Maybe it's a new talent, a new career, a new house, or a new personal look. Or it may be creating a painting, a play, or a book. You create when you plant the seed and start the garden of realizing your potential.

How are you going to cultivate your creation? Will you develop new skills? Change your daily schedule? You will need to establish ways to nurture your creativity and bring your full attention to it. It will take discipline, love, nourishment, presence, concentration, and time. When you create the garden, you are mindful of the soil, which needs amendment. We will dive deep into the process of amending the soil to help the roots push through. And once you have planted the seed, the cultivation continues as you water, fertilize, and tend the garden.

Then the celebration begins. How will you celebrate this process of cultivating and creating? Gratitude is a key method of celebration, and it can shift your life. You can also celebrate by sharing—sharing the fruits of your labor, your gifts, and your love. You see the first sprout, the cultivation continues, and life grows right in front of your eyes. The celebration grows as you see the fruits of your creation come to life, and you experience the joy of abundance.

If you look carefully, love is a part of every stage in the life cycle of personal growth. As you move through this book and the concepts presented, I invite you to reflect through the lens of love. Love for yourself and the beautiful potential that lies within you, waiting to flourish. When we look with the lens of love, we hold ourselves gently when the garden fails. The choice becomes: do I begin again or do I abandon my efforts? We can rebuild, this time learning from the lessons of the previous cycle. Too much fertilizer? Not enough water? We will explore how to evaluate our efforts and learn to keep the cycle going. Maybe we choose a different seed. Maybe we replant the seed again. Maybe there is a clearing. The important thing is to keep going. To keep living the cycle.

Whether our new abundance is noticeable or our cycle restarts, it's a continuum. How we approach this continuum is up to us. Will we try again when we meet hardship? Will we share our abundance? The spark that started this book repeatedly tried to find its way to the celebration of being written and published. It took a long time for the seed to sprout and to move past the beginning. It took a significant life pivot and perspective shift to give the seed the suitable soil and create the type of garden that would let it survive past the sprouting stage. Cultivation was the most grueling. Time and space, as we will explore, are ingredients needed to bring the garden to life. As I'm writing this book, my son is four years old, we live in a shared household with my parents, and there's a global pandemic. The challenges became the blessings, and closed doors became open windows. I let go and entered the stream. I stepped into the flow of the cycle. Now you hold this book in your hands, and you feel the joy of my abundance. The celebration has come to fruition. This life cycle is explored throughout the book.

The present moment is in the center of this cycle. No matter what stage of potentiality you are in, you are in the present. This wisdom of being *in the here and now* has been taught by many exceptional individuals. I have learned from many teachers in my pursuit to understand more about mindfulness. Their influences and backgrounds vary, yet they all point to the power of presence. They have bridged the concepts of mindfulness and meditation from specific cultures and consciousness into the hands of the everyday individual. Spiritual traditions have been calling us to recognize the impact of who we are in every moment of our lives.

My first introduction to mindfulness was through my yoga teachers, Laura and Bhava. I learned the power of restoration and nourishment through their Deep Yoga classes and gatherings in the grassy parks of their neighborhood. I was new to yoga when I began taking their classes at the local yoga studio. Slipping off my shoes, finding a spot to unfurl my mat on the floor, and soaking into the bliss of class became a weekly ritual. When I learned that they were offering a yoga teacher training and Vedic healer course, I promptly signed up so I could bask in their wisdom. I learned about being made of stardust and the beauty of breathwork. Most significantly, I learned to slow down and arrive in the moment.

The personal awakening that I experienced during my yoga teacher training led to my decision to take a personal sabbatical from work. During my six months away from the world of pharmacy, I attended a Vipassana meditation retreat, lived at Esalen as a work scholar, and learned the value of Karma Yoga at Mount Madonna Center. How does all of this relate to potential and creativity? The construct of life is about potential, the ability to change, heal, and manifest, just as the cells in your body constantly do. We are adapting, listening, and creating. We can incorporate these actions into our daily lives when we embrace the present moment.

Will we wake to the stories of our life? Will we travel through time and space to meet ourselves in this present moment? How do we synthesize the concepts of creating and bringing our potential into the world? For me, I needed something tangible. By utilizing the metaphors of the natural world and recognizing the similarities found in the life cycle of a plant, a human cell, and the stories of humanity, I was able to see a continuum in these layers of nature.

Life cycles are circle stories. Within the cycle, there is overlap. But, as with all circles, there is fluidity and movement between one stage and the next. They bring us back to our beginnings, teach us the importance of repetition, and represent the reality that we continually grow, adapt, and change. By embracing this life of personal growth, I hope you will transform what burdens you into a blessing.

Rings of Remembrance

The life cycles of our lives tell stories, and these stories carry lessons that inform us as we travel through life. The stories leave a mark on our lives; they leave rings of remembrance. Just as a tree has the imprint of experience held within its trunk, life leaves imprints on our bodies and souls. The grandmother tree I encountered reminded me that many cultures have stories about seeds. There was a scraggly aspect of her bark, held in an indentation of her trunk, that reminded me of Quan Yin, the goddess of mercy and compassion. It is with the graceful empathy I learned from this goddess and the gracious women in my life that I would learn to approach the stories, the marks, and the memories of the people I come into contact with as a pharmacist, coach, and human journeying through existence.

There are stories from Greek mythology, such as Persephone eating pomegranate seeds and their impact on the seasons, Native American stories about animals and their abilities to re-seed the forest, and the lotus seed of Asia and its ability to survive for hundreds of years and still germinate. Each story is influenced by the interactions of the seeds with the people and their cultures. So, as you connect with your seeds of potentiality, you will also connect with your roots and heritage.

When we learn of our heritage, our culture, we learn the stories from those who have come before us. These stories are like the rings held within the trees—these stories are rings of remembrance. Our personal experience is influenced by the communities and cultures we are a part of in our journey through life. By looking at the layers of life and these metaphors, it becomes apparent that the physical plant seeds of the world hold their genetic intelligence and carry their stories, just as we hold in our DNA the codes to our past, present, and future.

The people who have come before us, our ancestors, are an essential part of our heritage. I hold a special place in my heart for my grandparents. They have influenced who I am today through the stories of their lives and what they endured. Grandparents are amazing because they bear witness to the stories of others by sharing the wisdom of their life journeys. Their stories are recorded deep within and mark the stages of time. They have weathered brutal storms and seen times of flourishing abundance. Grandparents are an essential part of our communities and remind us of the potential that lies within. This understanding of her influence is how the grandmother tree became a pivotal part of my journey of self exploration. She was my witness, and she told me stories of what came before.

Life experiences and how we travel through them influence how we manifest our existence. Continuing with the parallel of the seed, we can learn from their travels. In nature, seeds can travel in many ways: flying, hitchhiking, going with the flow, and being transported. Flying in the natural world happens when the seed has wings. Think of the dandelion seeds you see on the cover of this book. These seeds adapted to be light and freely move about on currents of air.

The next method reminds me of running through fields as a child and discovering that my socks and shoes were filled with little hitchhikers. These seeds have attached themselves to your clothing, socks, or shoes to be taken to a new destination. Animal fur is another excellent mode of hitchhiking for seeds. These seeds reach their goals through perseverance and serendipity.

Some seeds float. One seed you may not think of as a seed is a coconut (seeds can come in a variety of unexpected forms). These seeds even travel the ocean currents and bless our beaches with palm trees, sometimes even floating from one island to another. Seeds may also float down rivers or streams, relying on the rushing current to speed them to their destination.

Seeds are also transported in ways that may feel a little too personal. This mode occurs when an animal eats the seed; the seed travels through the animal's digestive tract and arrives in a new location within a natural pile of fertilizer. Before you discount this mode of transportation, consider the times in your life when the situation called for you to make lemonade out of lemons. The sour, smelly, crazy times in our lives can often be the perfect breeding ground for something remarkable. Sometimes seeds must be digested before they can germinate, just as we must digest and work through our experiences before our dreams can take root.

One journey that impresses me is the seed of the giant sequoia tree. This seed grows only after a forest fire. Imagine being born from fire. Maybe you feel like you have been through the fires of life. When a tree survives a fire, it leaves a mark within the rings of the tree. The rings of the tree tell the story of its life. We, too, carry the story of our lives within our bodies. Just as the scar of the fire is imprinted on the ring of the tree, physical or emotional scars can be left on the tissues and memories of our existence. What is impressive about a tree is that it continues to grow beyond times of hardship. We can also grow beyond challenging times. And just as a tree, a plant, and a flower have seeds of potentiality, so do you. What seeds of potentiality lie within you? What is your seed story? The potential within you is like a seed just waiting to grow. We will explore how that seed contains the life force to bring what is needed to your life, to this moment, and how by tending to that seed, you will then celebrate its growth and magnificence.

As we continue this journey together, I will share stories of how my vision fast and life experiences shaped my perspective on life. You will see how seeds travel. It may not be the way you typically think of a traveling seed, but it's how the seeds of potential have traveled in my story. And I will share with you how they can travel in yours. Our journey through life makes impressions on our bodies, our minds, and our souls. These impressions are rings of remembrance. They do not have to hold us back or inhibit us from making changes. Just as a tree can grow through drought, storms, and fires, we can do the same. To promote our growth and personal evolution, we can continue to connect with our seeds of potentiality, personal life cycles, and rings of remembrance. The stories we carry inform our journey. They do not need to hold us back. We can hear the call, we can go into the unknown, and we can return with the gift of our presence to the life that is unfolding before us.

The Grandmother Tree Meditation

Your back is supported by the trunk of a tree, a tree that loves and holds you without judgment. It's strong and rooted soundly into the earth.

This is your grandmother tree.

She holds you lovingly in her arms, and you rest in her assurance.

A deep breath takes you within, and in your mind's eye, you can see the building block of life, a cell.

Your cells are breathing with her cells, and the symbiosis of this respiration fills your lungs with the life-giving air that restores you.

Breathe deeply.

Your awareness expands as the oxygen revitalizes your body. You connect with your potential—from the oxygen carried in your cells to support your breathing to the firing of your neurons that orchestrate the functions of your body. You are a symphony.

The music carries you to a point where you can reflect and look at the entirety of your life.

You see a circle, a pattern of events that evolve and turn with time.

In the center is the present moment. It is the center of everything.

A seed appears in your vision. It cracks open, and a glowing sprout unfurls from the shell. You hold the unfurling seedling in your hand and recognize that it needs planting.

You find a pot of fertile, soft soil and gently immerse the seedling into its new bed. With ease and care, you water the soil and place the pot in the sunlight.

A time-lapse movie begins to play, and the seed emerges as new growth. Your cultivation and care have brought forth life.

As the plant grows, you recognize the seedling to be a small oak tree. You take the young tree to a sacred place and plant it. The tree grows in the sunshine and weathers the storms. Its rings carry the stories of time.

The trunk of this tree supports the life of another. It becomes a grandmother tree, and the story lives on.

The light trickle of the water runs easily over the rocks. The brook follows a groove in the earth with a gentle flow that offers renewal to those who come to it. The music it offers is a melodic balm to those who sit at its edge. The babble that rises from the rhythm it plays is a meditation that transports the listener to a centered and grounded place.

In the space of tranquility, the brook invites the listener to enter.

Chapter 2

THE BABBLING BROOK

The cool earth grounded me as I listened to the sound of the babbling brook. There was a well-worn groove along the side of the bank that was just the right size for me to melt into. By stretching out and lying back, I was able to look up at the dance of the leaves in the tree as they played with the breeze. The water tickled my toes, and its babbling was like the joy of a young child. The faint hum of the brook had a message; I quieted my senses to listen. It was saying: You have arrived. Resting in the calming peace of the present moment, I had the sensation of being held by the reassuring surroundings of the forest.

My mind fought with ideas and tensions about what had gone right and wrong in my life. Did I make the right decisions? Was I on the right career path? What did I want to achieve in life? I am a goal-oriented person—always have been—and learning how to let go and relax into this moment was challenging. I tried to focus on the melody of the water as it slipped by with ease over the rocks and branches in its path. My mind was contemplating: How do I enter the next chapter of my life centered in my wholeness?

That night I fell into a deep sleep. I woke, disoriented to my surroundings. My heart was pounding, and I was certain a mountain lion had been in my presence. I heard the breath. I felt the heat of an unfamiliar creature. My body bristled with fear. The dream faded as I adjusted to the moment and felt the morning dew on my face. The mountain lion had visited me in my dreams. Her presence was strong and held a message. She was reminding me that I came on this journey for a purpose—to awaken my potential and release my fears. I recognized that confronting my concerns would remove the roadblocks and allow me to move toward a life of service and meaning balanced with peace and contentment.

Releasing

The vision fast was a time to explore the terrain of our interpersonal landscape. The work of Bill Plotkin, founder of the Animas Valley Institute, was the psychological backdrop for our exploration. He describes himself as a "psychologist gone wild" and shares the framework of his teachings in his initial book, *Soulcraft: Crossing into the Mysteries of Nature and Psyche.* "There's so much more to who you are than you know right now. You are, indeed, something mysterious and someone magnificent. You hold within you—secreted for safekeeping in your heart—a great gift for this world. Although you might sometimes feel like a cog in a huge machine, that you really don't matter in the great scheme of things, the truth is that you are fully eligible for a meaningful life, a mystical life, a life of the greatest fulfillment and service" (Plotkin 2009, 9). The institute he founded both trains wilderness guides and provides experiential explorations. The intent of these expeditions is described in their literature: "It supports us to develop what has become a rare achievement in the contemporary world—a healthy, mature ego rooted in our wholeness, not in our wounds" (Animas Valley Institute 2021).

Plotkin's work encompasses an exploration of subpersonalities within our psyche. One of the personas is a risk-averse people pleaser, and this is the "loyal soldier." In an interview about his book *Wild Soul,* Plotkin states: "What distinguishes the Loyal Soldiers from the other three categories of subpersonalities is that they try to keep us safe by inciting us to act small, to act beneath our potential or one-dimensionally so that we might secure a place of belonging in the world" (Plotkin 2021). The metaphor of the loyal soldier was something we explored with our guides in our preparation for the voyage into the depths of our souls. There are also lion tamers, inner critics, escapists, shadow selves, and wounded children. I identified with the loyal soldier and her dedication to people-pleasing.

Too often, we carry and live with our wounds. They influence our vision and perspectives in a way that colors everything we see. Moving from the orders of the loyal soldier to the whole and mature adult that I yearned to be would require me to release the conflict that waged within my psyche. While I continued to lie at the side of the bank, I imagined myself at the scene of war. I had struggled to reach a water source that would rejuvenate my aching body, my weary soul, and quench my thirst—not only my physical thirst for water but also my emotional longing for solace. The loyal soldier was fighting hard to maintain peace between my internal and external worlds.

On the bank of the gentle brook where I lay exhausted and depleted, I struggled with this surrender to accept the rejuvenation the forest was offering. I drew in a deep breath and allowed the sweet trickle of the water to continue to ease my tensions. My heightened senses relaxed, and I was calmly able to contemplate the conflict raging in my mind. What were the stories and the wounds that this soldier was holding on to? I listened to hear what the soldier had to say.

The loyal soldier stated the following as the conditions of war:

- Keep the peace.
- Do not rock the boat.
- Make everyone happy.
- Please others.
- Do not rebel.
- Follow the rules.
- Be successful.
- Make others proud.
- Do it right (aka Do NOT fail).
- Be safe.
- Do not take risks.
- Be responsible.
- Be polite even when you are hurt.
- Do what you are told.
- Do not make waves.
- Control yourself.
- Hide your expression.

Each thought and each rule created tension and angst. I saw how the mental holds created both physical and emotional stress. It was uncomfortable to hear these conditions that ordered how to live. What had given these statements the stronghold within?

There was a war waging, and the loyal soldier was winning. My life was full, yet I felt lifeless. I was looking for a way out when really what I needed was to go through the process of healing and mending my pain and despair. The war was not going to dissipate by my giving up. I knew this because I had tried, and the battle still waged on. It was time to inform the loyal soldier that the war was over. The soldier had fought the good fight, but it was now time to surrender.

The act of surrendering does not always represent defeat. To resolve this internal conflict, the act of surrender was a process of waking up. I realized that the "war" was something I created in my mind by positioning my thoughts against each other. The mental constructs of how things should be versus what society says clouded my mind. The persona of the loyal soldier was trying to follow a directive to set life straight and achieve peace by fighting for it. What if peace was present all along? What if, by letting go of this persona, my authentic self would rise up and meet the beauty of a life unfolding just as it was intended and be in tune with the natural forces that are beyond my personal control?

The simplicity and beauty of nature were transforming and releasing those holds. I imagined the soldier lying here at the bank waiting to be revived. Surrendering to this process that was arising organically in the moment was transforming my tensions as they melted into the earth. I connected with my breath and watched where it traveled in my body. The miraculous interchange of oxygen and carbon dioxide was happening every moment, and it was sustaining my life. At the time, I was not focused on food, errands, appointments, and my typical daily life activities. All I needed was my breath and some water. In this place, I had both.

You may not be at the edge of a calming stream surrendering yourself to the transformation of your soul, yet you may yearn to be living life from a renewed premise—a premise of hope and wholeness. You can look within and ask what conditions of war your loyal soldier is dictating. If you do not find a loyal soldier, you may encounter an inner critic or some other subpersonality that dismantles your wholeness and weakens your confidence. How do you dialogue with this aspect of yourself?

Life has a way of moving us through the daily grind at a pace that makes it challenging to find time to stop and say hello. Not only hello to the people who are moving through time and space with us, but hello to ourselves. Here in the forest, I was meeting myself from moment to moment in ways that had been hard to find in my fast-paced frenzy. I was looking for something different, and I needed the peace and serenity of the forest to connect with my true self and put the soldier at ease. If we are not in the woods, how do we find this quiet place for intrapersonal connection?

Methods of making this internal connection can feel sparse, distant, and unattainable. Since my pilgrimage into the woods, I have completed my master's program, married the love of my life, continued to work as a pharmacist, and given birth to my precious son. Any one of these attributes of life can be enough to keep me from connecting with myself. I have returned again and again to practices of self-reflection and self-inquiry. I find the practice of releasing my expectations to be at the core of maintaining an internal balance. How do we release expectations? By slowing down, finding a place and time for refuge, and connecting within.

I continued in my meditation of surrender on the bank of the babbling brook. How would things look different when I rose from this spot? Where would I go from here? How would I know that the changes I sought were taking hold in my life?

I would know that the war was over when I could:

- Express myself through art and dance.
- Change and pivot my career path.
- Be willing to be different.

- Accept that I cannot please everyone.
- Say no without feeling guilty.

These are my seeds of potentiality. Cultivating these concepts is a part of the fabric of my life. Art and dance classes enrich my life. My education and experience are woven into my work—both as a pharmacist and a coach—and I am fulfilled from the time I spend with others learning about their seeds and the unfolding of their lives. I am also learning and witnessing the unfurling of human potential as I watch my son grow. Decisions I make in parenting show that I'm okay with being different and not following the norm or current trends. Cultivating a young, curious mind has been an ongoing evolution of exploration and learning. Being a parent immediately taught me that I cannot please everyone, including my son. The hard lessons of boundaries and limits come into play for both of us. The pandemic taught me that my family's health and safety come first, and saying no became easy.

Each one of these seeds has blessed my life. Take dancing, for example. One group I connected with around the time of my vision fast expedition was a Nia dance tribe. This dance form is based on a nonimpact movement style that evolved to include neural integration into its methodology. Dance has always been an outlet for creative expression in my life. With this beautiful Nia tribe, I danced my way through meeting my husband, getting married, and a good portion of my pregnancy. I am confident my son's connection to music and movement started in the womb during these classes. This tribe of dancers decorated and celebrated my way into motherhood, from prayer flags and a birthing necklace to home-cooked food that nourished my soul.

Becoming a mom opened many new ways of knowing and connecting with myself. I let go of the opinions of others and listened to my innate wisdom. Moms-to-be receive advice from everyone when we choose to invite another life into the world, and it can be very overwhelming. I envisioned a loving filter to sift through the external input. My husband and I bonded over creating a safe and enriching environment to raise our son. Part of our parenting journey included expanding our circle to include my parents as part of a multigenerational household. This phase of our family life cycle has been one of growth and enrichment.

Each seed is living its life cycle. There are the moments of creation, cultivation, and celebration in each aspect of my life that are ever-unfolding, rebuilding, and animating its potential. What are your seeds? You can identify what you want to plant in your life by recognizing what is already within you that is yearning to grow. Do you want more joy? More adventure? Maybe you want to feel more content and at ease with the flow of life. Ways to connect with your seeds of potentiality are within reach.

Uncertain where to start? Create a virtual visit to a babbling brook, or choose another source of imagery and sound that transports you to a place of refuge. Maybe you find a babbling brook video on the Internet or download an app that guides you through a meditation practice. Try anything from music that revives your soul to silence. Experiment—and see what resonates with you. Find a place where you can melt into the moment, find stillness, and listen to the melody of life unfolding.

When we take time to pause, to retreat, even if it's just five minutes in our day, we open the door to a moment where we can say hello and connect with the individual that we spend more time with than anyone else: ourselves. Why is this connection so critical? When we lose the sense of who we are, it becomes challenging to know where home is. Not the physical house—this home is the dwelling place of our soul. The loyal soldiers and inner critics fill our heads with mind chatter that veils our true selves. As a result, we may become lost and confused. Staying in connection with our authentic self brings clarity.

As you release into the moment, consider what beliefs and blockages keep you from living your full potential. What are you called to in your life? It may be as simple as spending more time in nature or possibly spending more time on a hobby that brings you joy. Whether you want to cook more for your family or change how America eats, identify that seed that resonates within you.

When I connect with my true self, I recognize the boundaries, tools, capacities, and strengths that I have now:

- The ability to speak my truth
- The power to speak up for myself
- The permission to be authentic
- Emotional strength
- Creativity
- Passion
- Positivity

What innate capacities reside within you? Do you see that the seeds, the potential, and the ability to grow are already gestating within? To uncover these seeds and allow their potential to unfurl, you can tap into methods to:

- Release expectations.
- Release patterns or habits that do not serve you.
- Release the mind chatter.
- Release how you have been.
- Release the façade and come into awareness.

I left the loyal soldier at the bank of the brook that day. Of course, that persona emerges from time to time and reenters my consciousness. However, the imprint of the ability to release that thought pattern is still ingrained in my knowledge, and I can say again: The war is over. To reiterate this process of continually returning to our authentic self, let us take a moment to dive into each method of releasing.

Release expectations. To release expectations, first identify whose expectations they are. Next, ask yourself why you are trying to meet these expectations. What will happen if you do or do not meet these expectations? What is the motivation for the expectation? Developing a personal practice of self-inquiry will help you uncover the origin and intent of the pressures you are placing on yourself. I have learned a lot from talking about my contemplations with an inspiring group of people in a book club exploring authors' texts that stimulate self-reflection. One author who teaches and reflects on the process of surrendering to the flow of the universe is Michael Singer. In *The Untethered Soul: The Journey beyond Yourself*, he states: "The truth is that most of life will unfold in accordance with forces far outside your control, regardless of what your mind says about it" (Singer 2007, 10).

Release patterns or habits that do not serve you. There are a lot of resources for changing our patterns and habits. The one that spoke to me is Amy Johnson's *The Little Book of Big Change: The No-Willpower Approach to Breaking Any Habit.* She challenges us to consider the source of our habits: "But what if your habit has nothing to do with your personal history, psychological makeup, or the circumstances in your life?" (Johnson 2016, 65). When we recognize that our habits are not personal, they become easier to release. Amy's approach aligns with my values and speaks to the potential we hold for change. In her book, she describes a very gentle and organic change process, generated from within and thus realistic and lasting. She has taken her concepts and built the Little School for Big Change. Through the course material and live calls offered through her school, I see the life-changing principles that connect individuals with their humanity and their potential.

Release the mind chatter. Inner critics, monkey mind, an unwanted voice that endlessly torments us—however you define the thoughts that rattle around, they keep us from being at peace. Cultivating focus through art, journaling, gardening, or whatever brings you joy helps you move into the creative space of flow. I will talk more about this flow when we explore the flowing current. Tap into the wisdom of authors, mentors, and guides that inspire you.

There may be stories from your culture or your spiritual belief system that enrich and carry you closer to that sense of inner stillness.

Release how you have been. When I suggest "releasing how you have been," I'm referring to awakening to and accepting who you are in a way that brings growth and positivity. If you are asleep, you wake up to being more aware and involved. If you are in hyperdrive, look at relaxing. Consider aspects of yourself that you would like to view differently. What are you waking to? The need for greater self-care? Do you have a call to action for social justice? Connecting to your authentic self often shines the light on how you genuinely want to show up in life.

Release the façade and live in awareness. We often walk through our lives in a fog and do not understand why we lack clarity in life. Releasing the façade is a call to remove the layers that cloud our vision. What is the façade that we veil our vision with? The misperceptions that our thoughts and actions define us. Imagine knowing yourself well enough that you know when to say yes and when to say no. See the bigger picture by stepping outside of your ego and connecting with the greater needs of humanity and our planet. Your seeds of potentiality can be the genesis of your transformation.

To make space for these avenues of growth, imagine that you are standing at the edge of a cliff with the ocean below. You have brought with you a load of boxes filled with your accumulated frustrations, what-ifs, and illusions of how your life should be. You toss the boxes over the edge of the cliff, and you watch them free fall. The containers open. As these symbols of your internal hoarding plummet to the waters below, their contents are released. They merge, and the elements are no longer contained within.

What happens when we allow for this personal expansion? Do we feel more comfortable in our lives when we release the pressures and confinements of how we think it's supposed to be? How do we connect with our deeper self and recognize there is room for our evolution? As we venture on this path of personal exploration together, find time to be outside and observe nature. Whether sitting on your front porch, walking in the neighborhood, or hiking on a local trail, be present with yourself while you are held in the beauty of the natural world. Nature has a way of transforming and renewing us. It also holds surprises that wake us to the unexpected.

Awakening Potential

Sometimes we awaken with an unsettled feeling. Our old ways of being that we released were a blanket of security. Now, without this covering of familiarity, I felt vulnerable. In my dream during the vision fast, I was certain that I had felt the heat and scent of the mountain lion's breath. Those sensations prickled my skin and activated my nervous system. Do I flee to safety or stand my ground? Maybe I freeze and feign that I am dead. Whatever my body's reaction, I encountered a threat. It's the sensation of the edge of something new, something big and unknown. The sharpness of this uncertainty cut through my layers of protection and pulled me in a new direction.

When in your life have you felt this threat of being birthed into something new and unfamiliar? Consider the first cry of a newborn baby. The gasp for that first breath of air is immense and necessary. Being torn from the warm womb and the encapsulation of comforts into the cold new world is startling. When we are born into new situations, new opportunities, and new ways of being, it can be scary. There is an intensity to our awakening.

The biological responses of our body amplify the emotional intensity. Cascades of messages and signals elicit changes in our breathing and heart rate. As our muscles tense and we prepare to face the unfamiliar being, we are suddenly swaddled in the comfort of recognizing the threat is not real. So often, our internal emergency response system is activated by aspects of life that do not require this level of attention. How do we calm these innate reactions and live from a more centered state of being? Understanding more about our biology and the neuroscience of our brains can help unravel some of the complexity.

Diving into the Pandora's box of neuroscience may be daunting as new concepts and knowledge of how our brain works are constantly evolving. The beauty of this exploration is seeing the connection between the neurons firing away in our brain and the perceptions of our mind. Our brains are constantly assessing the potential outcome of any given situation, seeking what provides the greatest reward. The brain's ability to determine the value of any given opportunity is substantial. The brain has neurons whose primary communicator is the powerful neurotransmitter they release, dopamine. The function of these neurotransmitters is to relay messages and call other neurons to action. Dopamine neurons send signals that influence motivation, learning, and choice of action and, therefore, our ability to live out our potential.

When your brain is conditioned to know that entering the breakroom at work on Friday morning means DONUTS!, it will do everything in its power to get you there. The rush of eating the forbidden donut only solidifies the excitement of the hunt, and the sugar that surges through your body sends cascades of signals. The brain does not have a moral dilemma about the donut. Instead, it thinks eating the donut will improve the current circumstances, especially if we're hungry, sleepy, or moody. Thus, our state of mind influences the brain's value assessment.

This value assessment combines the need for immediate gratification and the drive for relief from a rumbling tummy, a poor night of sleep, or a heated conversation. The reality is that the dopamine neurons are not operating on their own. Other systems are giving their input based upon the stored memories of this "opportunity." The prefrontal cortex and the limbic reward circuit work in tandem, evaluating the potential outcomes of the behavior. At the front of our brain, where the prefrontal cortex resides, we have the slower, more complex thoughts evaluating the impact of the action concerning the future and the bigger picture. In the center of the brain is the limbic system, which is fast and furious. It works on impulse and is sometimes referred to as the reptilian brain since it's less evolved. The limbic brain, positioned to act when there is the rapid firing of signals, influences choice based upon the rate of communication from the dopamine neurons.

Additionally, our brain is highly attracted to new options. I can see this in my four-year-old, whose mood shifts with a new box of markers or a new book. Of course, there are other markers and books in the house, yet the excitement of something that has not been encountered before appears to have a higher value than the well-worn storybook or fading ink. This drive for novelty could be why a new restaurant or a trip to some place we have not previously visited piques our interest. Taking this new concept further, we can apply this to the rush of changing jobs, buying a new car, or going on a new adventure.

Knowing that our brain is constantly seeking rewards and new behavior may leave us wondering how we tame this pleasure-seeking walnut in our head. How do we make decisions? If something is not serving us, how does the shift to choosing differently manifest? The answer lies in knowing that we can influence the flow of these internal signals.

By slowing down and channeling our energy we move toward the focus of our intentions. Knowing that our brains are preprogrammed to seek immediate gratification, we understand the challenge of leaving the donut in the breakroom or sending greetings of kindness when we feel hurt. These are everyday decisions that the dopamine neurons orchestrate, and when we align with the melody—the rhythm we desire to follow through life—a shift occurs. Aware of the breathtaking complexity of our neural connections, we quiet our reactions and appreciate the internal networking of our brains. We can step back, return to the tranquility we experienced beside the babbling brook. We are calmed, and our senses are at ease. The brook can now lead us to larger tributaries and eventually to the rushing stream of life—we are ready to enter.

Entering the Stream

There is a moment when we surrender and float into presence with all that is around us. We are lifted and carried through the currents of life. We have entered the stream. Feel the weightlessness and the movement of the current. The tempo may change, speeding up and then slowing as the navigation through time and space adjusts to the curves and meandering of the landscape. Your whole being accepts the path, the current, and surrenders to the experience. This acceptance was the sensation I felt of having no expectations of doing anything other than simply being while fasting from the business of life during my time in the woods.

The essence of entering the stream is a process of acceptance. This is the moment when you grasp that there are aspects of life that you do not have control over. It's not indifference or apathy. Instead, it's an acknowledgment that the moment-by-moment purpose of life's flow is revealed as we live it. We can drift and move with ease as we ride the current. When we honor the life cycles of cultivation and creation, we celebrate life.

Balancing the concepts of surrendering to the flow with showing up to live life can be challenging. How do we release the reins and still recognize our responsibility? We explored this exact concept in one of my book club meetings while reading Michael Singer's *The Surrender Experiment.* In his book, Michael shares his personal experience of consistently surrendering to the flow of life. He was able to accomplish this by releasing personal preferences and recognizing the chatter of his mind. "My formula for success was very simple: Do whatever is put in front of you with all your heart and soul without regard for personal results. Do the work as though it were given to you by the universe itself—because it was" (Singer 2015, 133). His disciplined and consistent approach to life paved the path to success. When this success led to large-scale challenges, he stayed true to following the flow, and it carried him through.

We can also choose to follow the flow of life and reconsider how we encounter the rocks, the eddies, the bends and twists, and the cascades. Life is happening, and we are on this trajectory of continually moving forward. Time does not stop. How do we want to experience our daily routines? Can we see the small celebrations and learn from our mistakes? Is it possible that we are making too big a deal out of the direction we are heading, forgetting to look at the beautiful scenery we're passing? It's often hard to accept that life is rushing forward, and the degree of our control is not as significant as we think.

At the end of the stream is our transition from this world. Death is exceedingly difficult for us to accept. I will never forget the funerals of my loved ones. The first funeral I can remember was my grandmother's. I was fifteen, and I spoke to the crowd of more than thirty people. The next was for a teen suicide during my freshman year of college. It was so difficult to hear that a close high school friend had taken his life. Was this the ultimate example of giving up? Why wasn't my friend able to reach out for support? So many questions filled my mind as I contemplated his death. So to cope with my grief, I did an entire art project. I created an installation—a virtual closet where the viewer would enter this life-size space built from PVC pipe spray-painted brown and adorned with brown fabric. Inside the closet, there were words, a poem of despair written in glow-in-the-dark paint hanging from old wire hangers illuminated by a black light. There was a toy pistol on the floor, and the music that played was from the iconic rock band Nirvana. The key to this art installation was the fact that you could step through to the other side. To step into the grief and accept the totality of its despair and then experience the power of moving through life's experiences rather than running from them.

Movement through these difficult times is one way we enter the stream. Just as I did not close myself to processing the death of others, we do not have to close ourselves in times of hardship. When we give up, we shut down; we become apathetic and stagnant in our life—we lose connection with our life force. This world needs people who are alive and flowing with vibrancy. One example of someone living out the fullness of life is an amazing therapist who has transformed her grief into a life of service. Jennifer Allen's poignant story is portrayed in her book, *Bone Knowing: A True Story of Coming to Life in the Face of Impending Loss.* "I'm right there with him, until he stops speaking. Then I fall flat into this reality where such things don't feel possible. The pace I've taken, just to keep up with my life goes much too fast for such a heart connection" (Allen 2009, 183). Most of us can connect with a time in our life when the pace we live keeps us from dealing with the pains in our hearts. Lisa Gebo's endorsement of the book shares the depth of Jennifer's story: "Bone Knowing is about the intuitive wisdom we all have, but don't always heed. In Jennifer Allen's painfully honest account of her husband's struggle with cancer and his dying process, readers witness Jennifer's efforts to tune in and listen to her inner voice. There we find beauty and transformation, as well as selfishness, anger, old wounds, and guilt. Embracing all those qualities allows Jennifer to be wholly present for one of the most challenging times in her young life. By viewing Jennifer exposed, 'to the bone,' readers reap essential lessons on love and loss, relationship and renewal" (Allen 2009).

You choose your path and your response. Do you flow with the waters of life, or will you become stuck in a whirlpool of apathy? Our brains can do either. Conceptualize the immense potential held within the billions of cells in our body. Our expectations and perceptions strongly influence the potential of our biology, our soma. Our somatic experience is key in accessing our potential because our energy, vibrancy, and ability to be in our skin and live this life come down to an acceptance and appreciation of the interconnections of body, mind, and spirit.

One method of unpacking the power of our perceptions is to consider the placebo effect. As a pharmacist, I am familiar with research that compares the outcomes and weighs the effectiveness of therapies against a placebo in clinical trials. We often think of pharmaceuticals when the placebo effect is mentioned, yet the neuroscience behind the thoughts and biological responses attached to the perceived values of treatment is far-reaching. This evaluation of the estimated impact of a remedy can influence our expectations and alter our brain chemistry.

Pain relief is an excellent example of the placebo effect in action. An example from Wager et al. (2004) of the placebo effect was a little different than your standard drug trial because it demonstrated the impact our beliefs have when we perceive something will not have an effect. Imagine two groups of people receive a cream that is intended to provide pain relief. One group is told that the cream has active compounds that will penetrate the skin and provide relief. The other group is told that the cream is simply the base cream being tested without active ingredients. The cream is identical for both groups—it's simply a topical product without medication or active ingredients. The group that believes there is medicine in the cream that will provide pain relief will activate the neurons to send pain relief signals. In the group that does not have hope in the cream, the neurons will send increased pain and discomfort signals. This simplified example confirms our notions about the influence of external antidotes on the discomforts of life—we see the interplay between the thoughts of the mind and the messages manifested in our biology.

Is there a cure for this complexity? We can attempt to harness the wild thoughts that charge through our minds, or we can learn to let them filter through our awareness. The decision is yours, and the discipline involved in either path is significant. For me, the days of thought taming are coming to an end. I am entering the stream of my awareness and finding the flow of saying yes to life. The strain and pressures are less, and I am learning to embrace the path and the current that moves me. The babbling brook is a lovely place to enter the stream, hear the call, and surrender into life.

There are times in our lives when we hear the call. This call may be about changing careers, moving to a new place, or living life differently. It may also be the call to an adventure or journey that we have not taken before. I heard a calling when I decided to go on a vision fast. I had no idea what this time would hold and how it would impact my life. I knew I was at a juncture in my life where this opportunity was synchronous with my learnings in school and my internal explorations. I wanted to go deeper and discover more about my role and purpose in life. Finding our life purpose or calling can be overwhelming, and I needed a container for my exploration. Uncertainty of what journeying into the wilderness would hold shifted to curiosity and wonder about what I would learn and unearth about myself.

The Babbling Brook Meditation

You feel the coolness of the earth below you as you sit beside the babbling brook. The bubble and pop of the water tickle your ears. There is a rhythm and melody to the water that passes by. You feel heavy on the solid structure that supports you.

Slowly the concepts you hold that no longer serve you release through your pores and melt into the ground. The earth absorbs all that you no longer need.

You feel lighter. Ready to journey.

Your toes touch the edges of the cool, refreshing water, and a surge of joy runs up your spine.

The potential of a different path sparkles on the surface of the water.

You begin to feel as light as a leaf, and you slip in.

You are floating weightlessly on the surface, and you are at complete ease.

There is nothing you need to do. Just surrender to the gentle and supportive current.

As you flow along, you hear the melodies of the water and feel the sweet sway of the waters. All tension has been released, and you accept the flow. You relax and look up at the trees as you float along.

The sun dances through the leaves and the soft, delicate petals of the sweet blossoms.

Breathing in, you feel close to nature and your true self. You are connected and at ease.

Letting go of ideas, agendas, and expectations, you melt into the present moment. You see time floating by as you surrender to the swirl and flow of your life.

The warmth of the day feels new as the layers of winter bundling are shed. As you travel further, new horizons emerge, and the days lengthen.

You think: I am myself and in my element.

Taking in what feeds your soul and letting go of what is not needed.
Releasing.
Accepting.
Knowing.
You float freely with the musical current of the babbling brook.

It's the energy that rises and lifts.
The intense swirl and circulation of movement cleanse the air and make room for curiosity and exploration.
Time has left, and the only experience is the present moment. The pulse of bliss and joy populate the atmosphere and illuminate.
Innocent and expansive, it surges, slows, and gently carries the traveler.

Chapter 3

THE FLOWING CURRENT

The brisk morning air filled my lungs and my weary eyes slowly opened to the arriving dawn. Settling into my solo time in the wilderness, I'd managed to get some sleep in this unfamiliar spot on the earth. The sweet song of the birds filled the air, and I felt the promise of the day ahead. I caught my breath. What did the day hold? There was no agenda, no to-do list, no errands to run, and no work to accomplish. I was struck by the stark contrast between this moment in time and the days that filled my routine life. I typically ran on busyness, and now there was nothing to do.

I ventured down to the little brook near my solo spot. A swirl of breeze swept across my face, and the warmth of the earth held me. In this timelessness, I was transported and felt almost as if I were floating. In this reverie, I lost track of time, and I was released from its boundaries. A chill ran down my back, and my whole body relaxed.

There was nothing but this moment, and I was absorbed in nothingness and everything simultaneously. The gently flowing stream tickled my toes, the sweet sound of a bird tickled my ears, and the breeze continued to tickle my face. I breathed all of this into the depths of my existence. The moment was fleeting, yet the pause allowed the experience to sink into my cells. This place of bliss was both real and imprinted in my neural memory. And in this moment, I am comfortable with the uncertainty of life.

Allowing Uncertainty

What happens at the threshold between the comforts of familiar daily bustling and the uncertainty of times when our routines are turned upside down? Some encounter this juncture between a busy agenda-packed life and an empty schedule when they lose a job, face an illness, or find themselves in a global pandemic. I first experienced this screeching halt of activity on my vision fast. Now, years later, I provide career coaching to individuals whose familiar daily structure disappears when they leave their jobs or their jobs leave them. When the global pandemic fell upon us in 2020, many experienced a shift from the normal flow of daily schedules to varying degrees of uncertainty. The discomfort of stillness may arise when there is a lack of activities to keep our bodies and minds busy. How do we respond to times of inactivity? Does slowing the pace of life surface discomfort for you?

Slowing the pace of life provides the opportunity to be creative with the patterns in our daily life. Maybe you thought slowing down requires extra time. What if learning to be present in the life you're living releases the time-bound pressures of expectations? Evaluate how you spend your time. What do you prioritize? When we engage in regenerative activity—this includes rest—the energy to forge new paths and tap into our creativity becomes accessible. As we cultivate what we choose to focus on, the ability to flow with the current of life becomes more of a reality.

We all have our own stories of how we relate to, honor, and spend our time. It's a central theme for me in my struggles. I always seem to be short on time, and I always want to achieve more—I love to make a list and get everything crossed off. Unfortunately, my lists have become long and overwhelming. What if I were to give them up? Poof! Presto! Gone. I am still trying to work this magic in my life. However, it seems inconceivable not to have a method to track the upcoming items to accomplish. To remember the appointments, tasks, and deadlines, most people need something to keep their schedules organized. I've tried planners, apps, and calendars of various sorts. To discover what works best is to allow for experimentation. I found that I need a lot of flexibility, and the permission to skip days (or maybe even weeks and months) when writing things down is frustrating me more than helping. My favorite way to plan out the day is to have space to make doodles or draw pictures of the tasks and chores that need attention. I recognized that what I needed was more creativity and flexibility with how I charted my time. By holding compassion for myself and exploring my unique needs, I was resourceful. Creativity calls for adaptability, and I found that continually adapting to my needs gave me the room to grow and go with the flow!

To learn more about being flexible with time and to permit myself to slow down, I considered the advice of a dear friend who was exhausted by my drive to accomplish things. I will never forget one weekend when I was frustrated, again, that I didn't get everything done that I wanted to complete. My friend simply asked, "What are you trying to accomplish?" I listed seven to ten items. She looked at me and smiled. Did I think I could get all of that done? Upon honest reflection, I realized that trying to cross off everything on the list was truly not feasible. Why put all this pressure on myself? She suggested I pick one or two top priorities and accomplish those tasks and then take some time for rest and self-care. Maybe then I would feel less frazzled. I received this advice close to twenty years ago, and I'm still fully integrating this wisdom into my life. The lists are still too long, and I still try to do too much, as I constantly rearrange my priorities. What speaks to me the most in this struggle is acceptance. Accept that I am human, and to be genuinely present and effective in this life, I need to take care of the only life I have 100 percent responsibility for—my own. How do I move into the space of taking care of myself? By cultivating a sense of home within and being connected to the bigger picture.

There are times in our lives when we feel lost, and our internal compass only sees the unknown; the future is uncertain, and the choices before us seem daunting. At these times, we often put a lot of pressure on ourselves, and we become stuck. What if we found that the outpouring of our innate creativity can release us from the holds and bring us into the flowing current? Creativity allows us to generate resilience by tinkering with new ideas and concepts. We begin to explore possibility, and those seeds of potentiality—the ways we are yearning to be—become clearer. This description makes the juncture between the known and the unknown sound more straightforward than it is. I'm not discounting the complexities of the situations individuals, families, and communities face when life shifts in challenging ways. The point is that these situations provide the opportunity to connect with yourself, your internal strength, and your ability to change. You are still you, and through your choices, your interactions with the internal chatter of your thoughts, and the actions you take, you do have the potential to transform.

How we respond to times of stress is not only emotional but also physiological. Our body has innate systems to respond to the changes in our environment. The sympathetic nervous system is the one that developed to help us in times of danger: our fight, flight, or freeze response. And that is where we initially go when in distress. It's where I headed even in writing this portion of the book. The feeling of uncertainty is difficult for me to digest, and the woes of current world events eat at my ease and get under my skin. How do we reconcile this tension between known and unknown? Will we always respond in distress? What if we embrace the challenges? Words like acceptance and surrender float to the forefront of my mind, and the workings of my nervous system shift into the beauty of the parasympathetic nervous system, where I can rest and ruminate. The signals and the hormones shift the internal responses, and my body opens rather than bristles. I have spent a lot of time fighting or fleeing the unknown. However, when I reflect on my response and embrace the uncertainty, life begins to flow like a stream, and calmness carries me forward.

How do you accept the unknown? First, allow the feelings and sensations of uncertainty to move through you. Instead of battling fear or trying to run from it, use your awareness to calm the forces.

Second, walk through the fear with a serenity that allows the emotions that grip you to dissipate. This calm confidence rises from a connection with the constructs of life and the flow of energy beyond our singularity. Lastly, when we recognize the forces that are greater than our minds and emotions, we begin to break free.

When we surrender, we ride along with the current of life; we become one with the flow. This surrendering, however, does not imply that we are apathetic or unengaged. On the contrary, to stay "in the flow," we must remain alert, flexible, and respond to the shifts in the water. The pace may change from a stream to roaring rapids, and how we choose to engage impacts our navigation ability. The transitions and turns that we encounter become a part of our dance with the ebb and flow of life. Instead of resisting and feeling bound by the circumstances of life, we see life events as blessings moving us to new places and new opportunities.

One way to allow uncertainty to flow in our lives is to become curious. Curiosity shifts our perceptions and perspectives from doubt and fear to engagement. Children are excellent teachers on how to be curious. The relentless "why?" of their youth demonstrates a hunger to learn and know more. When we become inquisitive about our lives, we can explore how we respond to circumstances. Do we have blinders that make us set in our ways and restrict us to a narrow path? Or are we willing to be fascinated and pick up the rocks to investigate the icky and wriggly things below? Will we stand in awe of a rainbow? Will we chase bubbles with tireless joy?

By entering the playful bliss of childlike energy, let us explore how combining our awakening at the babbling brook with the process of allowing uncertainty connects us with our creativity. Creativity unlocks our potential and feeds our ability to grow. When we see creativity through the lens of helping us be more adaptable and find solutions to difficult situations, we also see its ability to help us heal. Creativity brings balance and flow to our lives. By approaching the issues in life from the position of our creativity, we can take the pressure off and make self-care accessible, attainable, and fun! By recognizing that we are innately creative beings, the need to look for something outside of ourselves to bring a sense of peace dissolves. We can utilize creativity to rebuild our responses, cope with change, connect with our sense of play, and discover our joy.

What do I mean by rebuilding our responses? This process is when we reframe, forge new paths, and build our resilience. For example, imagine you are building a block tower with a young child. Either the structure reaches a stability threshold, or the child becomes frustrated, and the blocks come tumbling down. As the adult, we offer encouragement and show the child that we can rebuild it. Not only can the physical structure be rebuilt, but so can the child's response to the problem. Our desire is for them to learn resilience and the ability to push through challenges. It's time for us to listen to this wisdom and apply it to our own lives. Whatever has fallen, crashed, been destroyed, or ceased to exist in your life—you can retool your response. See the opportunity to build anew. Recognize the potential for something to grow out of the pile of rubble. What grows from challenging circumstances may surprise you.

In the first chapter, I talked about seeds and their potential to grow and bloom into brilliance. The fate of a seed is uncertain. There is a natural process that must occur for the potential to be unlocked. One very hearty seed is the lotus. This seed can withstand the test of time. The plant has been known to still grow from seeds that are over one hundred years old. Once the lotus seed germinates, the plant pushes up through the muck and mire of the pond to blossom into its amazing performance as an absolute spectacle to behold. These flowers are a gift to the viewer as their large globes explode into bright balls of beauty. When we recognize that this same metaphorical potential is held within us—waiting to germinate and burst into being—our ability to move through the muck and thick goo of life is like the lotus. As Masaru Emoto states in his book *The Secret Life of Water*: "If you feel lost, disappointed, hesitant, or weak, return to yourself, to who you are, here and now and when you get there, you will discover yourself, like a lotus flower in full bloom, even in a muddy pond, beautiful and strong" (Emoto 2011, 141). As the lotus extends and reaches for the light, we too can hope and move forward simply by being ourselves and connecting with our inner strength and beauty. As we allow life to live through us, we rise through the circumstances, and our heart lightens.

When we connect with a sense of levity, the heaviness lifts, we find our ability to laugh, and joy floods our body. Circumstances may be the same, but the experience of chasing those bubbles, watching the stars come out at night, and wondering what it would be like to light up the sky like a firefly leads to childlike rediscovering. So often, when I talk about engaging with our sense of play, adults shut down and tell me that games and crafts are frivolous. To change the perspective of those who are hesitant, I like to try a game where the outcome is unknown. If you think about it, that is the excitement behind games, being present, and enjoying the unknown as it carries us into the flow state.

To explore the unknown and play with perspective, I have a game that I share with everyone. To play this game, you take three pieces of paper, cards, or envelopes and write "create" on one, "cultivate" on the next, and "celebrate" on the last. Then turn the three items over and shuffle them until you have no idea which is which. Then on this flip side, decorate all three with images and pictures that relate to what you want to create, cultivate, and celebrate in your life. If you're going to write about what you hope to see bloom in your life, decorate with words that represent your hopes and dreams. Don't worry about what you're putting on each one. Let the process unfold. When you have completed all three, you can turn them over to see what correlates with each word. Something you may have thought you were creating may be celebrated. You may cultivate a point of celebration in your responses. The point of this game is to loosen our linearity. It takes the pressure off when we see that everything is being created, cultivated, and celebrated as part of the continuum. These are all stages of our personal growth, and they are all happening in different aspects of our life at any given time. This life cycle of creativity, cultivation, and celebration is a part of our humanity.

We have more compassion for ourselves and others when we allow life to unfold naturally and actively engage in activities that restore us. Whether it's the playfulness of a game, the adventure of cooking a new dish, or the pleasure of a weekend getaway, we receive the gift of renewal. By recognizing the innate need for rejuvenation, we accept the need to slow down and deeply experience the life we are living. By celebrating the things working in life and honoring them with gratitude, we gain insight into moving forward. Creative energy is a driving force in life. Creativity is the seed—the abundant energy that brings forth new ideas and ways of being in the world. By connecting with our creativity, we can move beyond the way we have approached problems in the past and allow the uncertainty that brings new opportunities to ignite passion and motivation in our lives.

Creative Energy

We have found the catalyst for immersing ourselves in a focused pursuit of wonder when uncertainty prompts curiosity. One of my fellow travelers on the vision fast was the curious sort. His fascination with the terrain pulled him from his solo spot into exploring the land. He connected with his inner child and allowed himself to go beyond the construct of our vision fast to find his journey of exploration. When we gathered to share our stories, his stories clearly showed that he was destined to find his soul path in life. He had been raised to live by the beat of his drum, and he had done that during his time in the wilderness.

Finding our rhythm, one that sustains and motivates, is a source of energy renewal. How does this happen? When we connect with the skills, talents, and activities that come naturally, our navigation through the world is more explicit. The more insight we have into these internal resources, the more we can recognize how to refill and replenish our inner well. How do we develop methods of self-care? How do we know the level of our internal reservoir? We will explore these terrains and discover how to quench our thirst in the joy of abundance. But first, let's find our fire starter.

Each of us has a passion (or even several) that sparks the kinetic energy to pull us into a state of flowing concentration. Our enjoyment of these passions comes from an internal origin, a wellspring that offers a sustainable energy source and helps us find our flow. Once we tap into this source of motivation, any barrier to acceleration is overcome. It's in this state of bliss, where we relate to our joy, that the framework of time shifts, and we enter the flowing current.

The concept of flow first became popular through the work of Mihaly Csikszentmihalyi. This Hungarian philosopher studied the creative process in just over ninety individuals from different walks of life and backgrounds. He identified in his subjects an internal construct that was consistent with the ability to fall into absolute bliss with the work or activity at hand. He determined that their enjoyment of life came from an internal, sustainable source. The individuals were active in pursuing clear, attainable goals that were appropriately challenging in relation to their skill set. His research revealed that individuals who could enter a state of flow increased their creativity, which led to happier and healthier lives (Csikszentmihalyi 2013).

For me, what is foundational about his work is that it translates creativity into an organic process that rises from within. We all can create. Being in the flow unlocks potential and unleashes the energy to put a sustained focus on the goal of our creative process. As Mihaly Csikszentmihalyi states, "Flow helps to integrate the self because in that state of deep concentration consciousness is unusually well ordered. Thoughts, intentions, feelings, and all the senses are focused on the same goal. Experience is in harmony."

(Csikszentmihalyi 2009, 41). Our internal integrations and focus give rise to this harmony.

Our seeds of potentiality hold new concepts, pathways, and actions, allowing life to burst forth and grow. The creative energy that rises when we challenge stagnant energy with the power of potentiality is magical. As a mother and one who experienced the challenging birth of her child, I see the essence of this cultivation of creative energy in the process of bringing forth life. Yes, birth is natural, and it happens every day as the earth spins on its axis, yet it's miraculous. It's a miracle born of uncertainty and potentiality. The inherent capacity to bring forth new life translates into other areas of life as well. The idea that has been living within you can be born.

The ability to give birth is profound and is often a spiritual experience. For example, this book is the result of a nine-year gestation that pushed through and gasped for its first breath amidst a global pandemic. I still utilize the journal I started at the conception of my business, Create Cultivate Celebrate. My business was born out of original thoughts and ideas that have now merged in this narrative. Bringing together the ideas, concepts, and inspirations that fuel our dreams into a meaningful structure can be challenging. Being creative can help us learn how to get through the tough times. Cultivating and completing a project fueled by generating and synthesizing concepts makes it more feasible to learn skills and tools that translate into innovation that can spill over into all aspects of life. You can connect creative energy with the rumination and attention needed to move past any barriers and cultivate personal growth. And celebrating both failures and success on the journey makes it even more enjoyable. This book is the result of a cycle of seed thoughts being birthed through creativity, cultivated by devotion, and celebrated consistently. And it carries a message that insisted on emerging into the world: You can create, cultivate, and celebrate your dreams.

What is the creative process? Many writers have attempted to answer this question. The answer is unique to each person. In this book, we are using the lens of potentiality. We each have the potential to manifest something from nothing. We cook food, choose our route to work or the store, and develop patterns for navigating daily life. Our creativity is at work in each of these activities. As a verb, Merriam-Webster defines "create" this way: "to produce or bring about by a course of action or behavior" or "to bring into existence." Creating is about bringing forth something new; it's the unborn potentiality that gestates within you. This unevolved aspect of your life may be a quality you would like to experience more of or perhaps it's an inherent skill that you've neglected.

I love shaping my understanding by using metaphors from nature and the physical world around me. The potential held in one cell speaks of creativity, and nature does "flow" effortlessly in this microscopic building block of life. Each organelle pulses with energy and automatically reads the DNA, constructs proteins, and keeps house. The active engagement of our bodies on a second-by-second basis is fascinating. Numerous systems are relentlessly running to keep our systems going without us even thinking about them. How do we translate these concepts into finding your creative energy? By trusting the innate ability your body and mind possess to generate new ways of doing things.

What activities do you find that generate an effortless spark of attention? It may be your devotion to expanding concepts, initiating projects, or leading teams at work. Some people gravitate toward the arts and enjoy painting, writing, singing, and numerous other forms of expression. Others find flow in a sports activity or hobby, and still others in the tending to their gardens. The list is expansive. What is consistent in all these pursuits? The generative energy comes from being active. There is a current flowing through you that produces the focused concentration. When we feel this seamless flow, we have entered the stream of creative energy.

Creative flow is based on neurobiology. Our brainwaves transport us to a place of daydreaming, and in this lucid state, our potential pours forth into joyous and effortless productivity. In this natural state of creation, people report that they often lose a sense of who they are. They merge with their activity of focus and lose track of time and space. Researchers have found that the medial prefrontal cortex (MPFC) of the brain houses our sense of self (Heatherton 2011). It's possible that in the state of flow, the MPFC shuts down, and the barriers blur between the concept of self and the object of focus. "Furthermore, there appears to be support in the literature for a particular neurocognitive activity pattern for flow induction in which expertise and flow studies appear to show a hemispheric shift away from the frontal left evidenced by a resulting reduction of left frontal activity and an increase in frontal alpha while facilitating a greater allocation of neuronal resources to the visual-spatial processes of the right brain, thus resulting in higher levels of performance" (Gold 2020, 13). To simplify, our creative, free state takes over the brain, and the inner critic that works in conjunction with our "top-down" thinking takes a break. With the critic quieted and our tendency to overthink things on hold, our confidence in our natural capacity for creativity can build. Freed from self-doubt and ego, a harmony of symphonic signals arises in the brain.

The cascade of neurotransmitters and neuropeptides playing the various notes are dopamine, serotonin, norepinephrine, endorphins, and anandamide. These biological chemicals produce feelings of pleasure, promote concentration, and influence our creative abilities. Take anandamide, for example. This chemical is based upon the Sanskrit word *Ananda,* which translates to bliss, joy, or happiness. Thus, the presence of this chemical explains why we feel peaceful and content when we are flowing with the current.

Endorphins are another orchestrator of this creative flow experience. These biological signals have made a name for themselves in their ability to be a natural pain reliever. The release of these neuropeptides may explain why not only our brain is tuned in to our activity of focus, but our body is at ease and present as well. Releasing our hold on life and entering its natural flow frees our ability to be creative. As we have discovered, creativity is a catalyst for moving past the barriers and shifting into the realm of cultivating life with a momentum that sparks a continual life cycle of personal growth. All time culminates in the present moment—the cycle spins continuously—and we joyfully lose track of the obsession with the past and future. Instead, we learn to inhabit our lives fully in the now.

Timelessness

Timelessness is realized through mindfulness and meditation. It's the practice of coming into the present moment, coming into the now. As we live out the life cycles of each generative thought, concept, and project, we begin to see that the cycles overlap and circulate. At the center of everything is the present moment; it is now. Connecting to the present moment is a tether to our humanity—our feet standing here on this earth experiencing life just as it is. This experience is the beauty of allowing uncertainty and the forces of creativity to move through us.

Trying different approaches to meditation can be helpful when exploring what form of meditation will work best for you. The method that resonates and works may shift with the changes and flow of life. There are times when a walking meditation sustains me as I connect with the sounds of nature and the fresh air. Other times, the deep quiet of the early morning allows me to find stillness within. Finding a way of centering and quieting your mind is a personal journey. It's not something to strive for or achieve; just see what unfolds for you. Let go of accomplishing and just be.

In the flowing current of our creative energy, we connect with the flame of passion and expression. When we lose track of time, creative energy translates into a flow that carries us over the rocks and around the curves of our life stream. Creativity takes us over waterfalls, plunges us into the deep, and surfaces us again. To be in this flow, we surrender to the process. I'm personally transported when I engage in process art. The focus of this approach of artistic expression is on the process of making art rather than the final product. In my expressive arts courses, I learned the importance of being in the moment and experiencing my process of making and creating. The beauty of allowing something to rise out of the moment-by-moment experience rather than being focused on the goal of producing is freeing. This liberating method of choosing the color that is needed in that moment, the line that needs to go just this way, or the images that exactly reveal what is being felt feeds the soul.

Sharing my enthusiasm for this approach to artistic expression transports me back to a course I took at Esalen called Painting from the Source. Aviva Gold is the creative medicine woman who developed this approach to process art. Her passion and excitement for the methodology of connecting the participant with "Source" are evident in her teaching. She guides individuals as they process life by painting their essence on paper. The course evoked deep images to arise and provided a transformative environment for self-expression. "The Source infuses the Creation that we humans reenact whenever we ourselves create. The Source is chaos within order, order within chaos, constant change and flux. It's itself the process of evolution. The Source demonstrates its sounds and logic through music, myth, and song; its movements through dance and athletic skill. Poetry and literature are its speech. And images—painting, color, and sculpture—are its many portraits" (Gold 1998, 9).

In addition to process art, activities like Tai Chi, yoga, writing, and listening to relaxing music have the potential to transport us into the space of timelessness. Be the chemist of your internal alchemy and find the bliss of being in the flow of life. Connecting with this place of peace in your life is more important than completing the to-do list or earning the approval of others. Give yourself permission to recharge, and you will find that it energizes your life in ways that "getting it all done" will never provide.

Imagine experiencing your entire system slowing and floating through an activity. Your shoulders relax, the orchestra of neurochemical notes shifts to a melody that supports ease and relaxation, and a chill runs down your spine. Melt into this space and allow your body to tingle with the release of knowing the wonder and joy of internal peace. Put on your imaginary lab coat, your symbol of curiosity and inquiry, and take yourself to the yoga mat, the outdoors, your journal, or simply to your breath. Ride the currents that rise and find what dissolves the tensions and stress.

What pain or tension are you carrying? What holds you back from releasing into the timelessness of the flowing current? The human condition is filled with complexities that often result in discomfort and disease. When an individual is experiencing physical pain, it's often difficult to find the means to move into this creative, flowing bliss that I am describing. Fortunately, traditional medicine is opening to new opportunities and innovations by releasing the constructs of treating pain with something you take—a pill or a remedy—and moving into new modalities that help individuals transport into this realm of timelessness.

One of the new treatment modalities that engage the mind in an alternative method for pain treatment is virtual reality (VR). "Two words often used with VR are 'immersion' and 'presence.' Defining these terms can help explain how VR functions. 'Immersion' is an objective term that describes the amount of sensory input the VR system creates. 'Presence' is a subjective value of the illusion one experiences when using the system. While separate values, an increase in immersion often leads to an increase in presence felt by the user" (Gupta 2017, 152). These concepts align with pursuing a rite of passage in the wilderness—being immersed in nature and fully present. When the individual is unable to travel to the forest or the natural landscape, what if they could be virtually transported there?

From my pharmacist lens, I was intrigued to learn what chemical reactions in the body were producing the profound outcomes of pain relief for patients treated with VR. Our brain is powerful, and the thoughts we think feed the pathways that carry the signals to the pain receptors throughout our bodies. The key is where attention is placed. "The capability of VR to reduce pain has mostly been attributed to active distraction. One main rationale is that attention is required for pain and exists in limited supply; therefore, diverting attention can reduce the resources available for processing pain" (Gupta 2017, 152). The evidence supporting the use of virtual reality compelled the hospital where I work to open two beds dedicated to this treatment modality. This act may seem like a small gesture, but in the larger scheme of allopathic medicine, opening to alternative approaches of healing signifies a more significant shift in our paradigms of healing. We, too, can shift our paradigms as we seek healing modalities to address our physical, emotional, or spiritual pain.

Guided visualization is a method, a useful tool, that is accessible in daily life. I can transport myself back to the babbling brook or the comfort of the grandmother tree anytime I want. To enter those places, I surrender to the moment and let go. I am swept by the stream of the neural imprints on my memory and allow the visualization to relax me and ease me into the flowing current of these joyful sensations.

When we allow ourselves to surrender and enter the stream of guided visualization, we awaken to the bliss of our neural networks transporting us through the fabric of the images, sounds, and experiences that are woven together. As you continue to practice with this modality, connectivity will strengthen, and you will be able to access this virtual reality anytime and anywhere. This gain in experiencing the imagery and sensations beyond the current physical state is the beauty of the virtual world. You do not have to be physically present on your favorite beach to access the freedom that you can find there.

The beauty of guided visualization is that you can tailor it to your needs. It's portable and can travel with you. The neurochemical symphony we explored in the previous section that looked at the cascade of chemicals released in the "flow" revealed the connection between the state of focus and the body's physical response. The harmonious melody of molecules modulated during guided visualization, meditation, and mindfulness create a positive biochemical effect. Some orchestra members increase their tone while cortisol is calmed and epinephrine is quieted. This release of neurochemicals allows the body to enter a space of rejuvenation and restoration. Serotonin signals a sense of rest, peace, and fulfillment. At the same time, the release of the hormones DHEA (dehydroepiandrosterone) and melatonin correlates with improved health and vigor. The music of the flowing current impacts your state of well-being.

Consider what holds you back from entering a sense of timelessness. Are you living in the future or stuck in the past? I know that I have spent a lot of time doing both. Time-traveling in our minds can rob us of the beauty of what is unfolding right in front of us. Recently I read the story of a pharmacist who was sharing her gratitude for her 101-year-old great-grandmother. She reflected on how this wise woman found joy watching the squirrels from her front porch and was pleased with a visit from family members. She doesn't know much about social media and isn't worried about posting or not posting for others to like or comment. This wonderful great-grandmother is living life in the present moment. What brings you into the now? Our existence, our being, has been carried and transported through time. When we recognize that we will move through time regardless of what we do, maybe we can catch a glimmer of the beauty of just being.

My wilderness retreat created a sacred time for me to be in the bliss of the moment-by-moment observations of the creatures, plants, and movements of the sun. The shift of the air currents on my skin was the gentle caress of life, calling me to live my life—not from a place of expectations, but from deep connectivity to my authenticity and aliveness. Flowing with the current of my creative energy, I allowed uncertainty to unfold. Finally, my back resting against the grandmother tree, I took in a deep breath and sank into the timelessness of the present.

The Flowing Current Meditation

Find yourself slowly shrinking. You are transforming into something beautiful and awe-inspiring. You are becoming a seed of hope.

You are a dandelion seed wished into the current of the air. You swirl and ride the energies of the atmosphere with ease and grace.

Feel the ebb and flow of your journey as you softly land upon a leaf in the babbling brook. Finally, you are swept down the calm waters, safe in your vessel.

The energies of the voyage are all that you feel. You surrender entirely to the sensations of the moment. Nothing else exists.

You feel the vast expansion of your essence.

You are free.

The air gently lifts you from the leaf in a sweet reverie of bliss. As you take flight, the energy of all that exists carries you to two warm hands, cupped, waiting to receive.

You land in the palm of your own hands.

You are held.

There is a dance that dances us.
She embodies our whole being.
Authenticity flows from the rhythms, connections, and melodies she births.
Her timing is impeccable, and those who follow her lead fall into step with the patterns and sequences of life.

Chapter 4

THE DANCE OF SYNCHRONICITY

Prior to our arrival at our individual solo spots, there was a dance in the woods that marked the time for us to select our vision fast check-in partner. The purpose of this partnership was to have someone else who was out in the wilderness aware of our location and in tune with our state of safety. There were only four of us. To avoid any awkward selection issues, each of us stood blindfolded in four separate corners of the field. Then the guides told us to slowly walk toward the middle of the clearing until we bumped into someone. This person would be our partner. I tied my dusty bandana over my eyes and slowly moved toward what I perceived to be the center of the grassy expanse. It was an awkward movement, and my trust in the process was tested. I was relieved when I bumped into another human being and recognized the exercise was over. My partner was the perfect match for me (of course), and days later, I would find that she and I supported one another in ways that aligned with how we needed to experience our time in the wilderness. I realized that the check-in partner selection process was a game of synchronicity.

Each day my check-in partner and I created a marking of stones, leaves, and other found objects in a new pattern to indicate we were still alive and well. If there was no sign of the other having "checked-in," then the partner was to go to base camp and seek help. I recognized that having this sense of security allowed me to relax into my process and trust the melodies of the forest to guide me on my mission to connect with the deeper realms of myself. Having a daily ritual of creating a rock tower or mandala of leaves to signal to another that I was safe and secure made me reflect on how travelers and adventures have used aspects of nature to guide their paths and help them feel connected when traversing the unknown.

One of those guideposts is the North Star. The North Star has been used for centuries by those crossing unchartered seas and unfamiliar territories. There is comfort in looking into the night sky and seeing the bright star that provides a constant guidepost as one finds their path. It provides a point of alignment and direction. I gazed up at the North Star that night from the comfort of my sleeping bag and felt supported by the fabric of the universe that was dancing to the melodies and synchronicities of life.

Alignment

At the time of my pilgrimage in the woods, I was working on my master's in counseling psychology, and we were studying the work of Carl Jung. In his work as a psychologist, Jung had a fascination with synchronicity and studied it extensively. In his book entitiled *Synchronicity: An Acausal Connecting Principle,* Jung quotes Lao-Tzu:

> Because the eye gazes but can catch no glimpse of it,
> It is called elusive.
> Because the ear listens but cannot hear it,
> It is called the rarefied.
> Because the hand feels for it but cannot find it,
> It is called the infinitesimal…
> These are called the shapeless shapes,
> Forms without form,
> Vague semblances.
> Go towards them, and you can see no front;
> Go after them, and you see no rear (Jung 2010, 71).

Our ability to taste, touch, feel, hear, or see the forces that weave together the occurrences that make up the fabric of life may seem intangible. However, trusting that the layers are coming together in perfect time and space allows us to move forward even when we cannot see where we are heading.

Cultivating the garden of our soul with this level of trust creates a vibrantly full and blooming life. Old patterns are released and new potential awakened. Use your creative energy to flow with the current of life and join the dance of synchronicity. Tune your awareness to the tonalities of life and be transformed by the magic of the rhythms and connections that rise by following the melodies. First, align with a positive and supportive network that reinforces your ability to care for yourself and find replenishment. Next, find your path that brings contentment and joy. Finally, listen to the melodies that feed your sense of aliveness. Now you are ready to join the dance of synchronicity and experience the satisfaction of falling into step with the natural patterns and sequences of life.

Being mindful of how to align ourselves with positive energy and activities that are life-affirming, we learn new ways to creatively address the obstacles we encounter. How we orient ourselves in the river of life influences our flow through the waters and currents. Affiliations that support our values and our authenticity build the connections that carry us in the direction of our deeper selves. When we partner with people, communities, and causes that spark our inner joy and passion, it bolsters us for making an impact. We begin to contribute to the larger collective from a renewed wellspring from within.

In writing this book, I connected and reconnected with social and environmental issues that I value. The grandmother tree wants us to feel connected to our heritage—both our cultural heritage and the history of the earth. When we explore nourishment in the turning of the soil, I will introduce the need to replenish our physical bodies as well as the soils of the planet. And when we quench our thirst in the joy of abundance, I will share the true value of water and the importance of honoring the water cycle. But first, I want to continue to deepen our understanding of the relationship between seeds and potentiality. "Seeds know how to softly open, as gentle lovers in love, they know how to silently work in harmony and total gratitude, as humble spiritual masters. They know how to create beauty and strength, as only true artists can do, nothing can stop their expression" (Shiva 2014, 73-74). It's not until the seed is planted that the potential held within can unfurl and express itself. I saw this soft opening of potential in the artistic, spiritual masters at Shakti Rising in San Diego during my yoga teacher training. Shannon and her team of amazing women created a sanctuary for the feminine to rise and manifest in pure beauty. My experience connecting with this soulful group of women deepened my exploration of authenticity and the spark that connects us with the calling of our soul.

Shakti Rising is an energetic organization of women centered around connecting individuals with the joy of aligning body, mind, spirit, and heart with the powerful energy that resides within everyone. They have numerous classes that offer support—from learning more about being good stewards of money to how best to tend to the soul. The class I took at Shakti over a decade ago was focused on resilience and self-care. At the time, I was new to many of the concepts and ideas that were being shared with me. This course expanded my vision of what integrating the layers of the physical, emotional, and spiritual realms looked like in life. Where are classes held and communities forming that support your soul? Seek out positive, life-affirming affiliations that will cultivate your growth.

Connecting to the larger framework of supportive communities builds a structure to hold us as we delve into the work within ourselves. Balancing the external and internal environments of our lives is crucial. To tantalize your imagination, follow me into a beautiful remembrance of a favorite self-care routine. See the soft swirling sea circled below as you stand at the ocean's edge. The vigorous salty air of the sea is a powerful place of renewal. The refreshing cool air and the far-reaching view to the horizon awaken us to an expanse of possibilities. I encountered this when I made a daily morning pilgrimage to the sparkling sea to reset the day and connect with my purpose. What daily pattern of taking time for renewal to strengthen your reserve can you create?

This renewal of personal fortitude was what my daily early morning pilgrimage to the ocean provided. At the time, I was living in a quaint little cottage in Carmel, California. It was a quick drive down the hill to the ocean. I had a spot where I clambered over some rocks to witness a pool of water that fascinated me. The daily tides changed the terrain and reminded me that the landscape of my life would change from day to day and season to season. Pairing my morning reflection to my love of the ocean generated an automatic pause for daily renewal. You can create this sacred time for yourself by considering what resonates with you. Maybe it's a morning walk in your neighborhood, or it could be a warm cup of tea or coffee in a quiet spot in your house. Then, pair the joy of that activity or place with a time of personal renewal. Combining an activity that brings you joy with a dedicated time for yourself will strengthen the neural networks that call you back to that pairing. Making time to recharge is essential to maintaining our ability to follow the flowing current of life.

Another way to align with our creative flow is to contemplate how we address the daily issues, problems, and practical matters that can disrupt our energy and creativity. One of my favorite activities for breaking out of linear thought patterns is using something called a mind map. The resources available and the formats for mind maps are numerous. Typically, you start with a central idea and then expand it in various directions to break down the attributes of the concept you are exploring. It's important to be organic in your process, allowing one idea to flow to another. I recently made one of these maps to explore the concept of health. In the center of the paper, I wrote down the word "health" and drew a circle around it. I then recognized that health is broken down into the physical, emotional, spiritual, and social aspects of life for me. I drew ellipses around each keyword and had fun using various colors for each subcategory. Then, I considered what was fundamental to achieve health in each of these areas. For physical health, I identified that exercising outside in nature was deeply important; this call to the natural environement was congruent with my spiritual need to connect with the trees, the song of the birds, and the shifting landscape. Between the bubbles for physical and spiritual, I wrote the words "time in nature" and drew arrows from these two attributes to those words. When I looked at the social realm, I reflected on my weekly book club. This community of like-minded individuals was serving my desire to connect with others. Arrows from the social, emotional, and spiritual bubbles all pointed to the subconcepts of finding my community and connecting with others—this all arose from being a part of the book club. As I unraveled what was important in these various domains, I saw a strong web of concepts and ideas on the paper. Taking care of my health no longer seemed nebulous or unattended, and I recognized that I was nurturing all these facets of my well-being. What aspect of your life might benefit from creating a mind map?

How do you contemplate maneuvering through obstacles and issues encountered in life? Sometimes to understand an obstacle, we need to dig deeper and go below the surface. Although I love thinking in abstract and nonlinear patterns, I learned the importance of analyzing and improving workflows as a pharmacist. These are generally linear progressions, with one step leading to the next to improve efficiency and efficacy. Creating these patterns of repetitive tasks to ensure the accuracy and safety of medication distribution has been a rewarding part of my career. Groups of medical professionals and I analyzed workflows looking at the potential breakdown points and where an error may enter the equation. This process is called *root cause analysis*—the purpose of this methodological tool is to look deeper and understand where the systems failed. The problem, or "error," is identified as what is seen—this is the tree in the construct of root cause analysis. The source of the error is hidden in the roots. The roots are the contributing factors and underlying issues that lead to the problem and cause the error, but they are often not apparent at first look. Just as roots are underground, the genesis of the error may be concealed. Unearthing the actual cause of the error may require some digging. I learned that the human component of the patterns and sequences that lead to failure is not always fully supported. To remedy points of weakness, efforts to bolster and improve both the systematic and support functionalities of the process can help with error prevention. Therefore, both the internal and external domains of our life need to be tended to and integrated. Just as the physical, emotional, and spiritual layers of ourselves are intertwined, so too is the interplay between our personal experiences and the occurrences of the world around us.

How do we find support to improve the workflows and patterns of life? We each have different ways of solving problems, creating habits and routines, and completing tasks. While I was working as a performance improvement pharmacist to better understand this juncture between humanity and striving for safer systems, I studied *To Err is Human: Building a Safer Health System.* "The problem is not bad people, the problem is that the system needs to be made safer." (Institute of Medicine 2000, 49). This crux of the problem is true throughout our societal systems. I want to take the concepts learned in my professional work as a pharmacist and develop strategies to support our humanity. How do we find solutions that protect and bolster the weak points? When faced with issues and problems in our lives, we can conduct our own root cause analysis to see what is under the surface. Where are the breakdown points for you? Do not overthink the issue and get pulled into the confusion. Bring the curiosity of the child or scientist that we connected with into our contemplations regarding the flowing current. Be open to what you discover. Dig deeper into the roots. Recognizing the patterns and sources of breakdown through an objective observational lens may help when you're looking for solutions. Strategic planning is something I try to help others develop in their attempt to be at peace with problem-solving in the present.

One solution is to pair activities together for reinforcement. I introduced this concept when sharing about my daily trip to the seaside. In that example, I was coupling the love of the ocean with taking time out for myself—I was reinforcing a new healthy habit. What do I mean by this concept of coupling or pairing activities? Neurobiology teaches us the axiom that neurons that fire together, wire together. Donald Hebb explored the neuropsychology behind this phrase in his book *The Organization of Behavior: A Neuropsychological Theory* in 1949. "When an axon of cell A is near enough to excite cell B and repeatedly or persistently takes part in firing it, some growth process or metabolic change takes place in one or both cells such that A's efficiency, as one of the cells firing B, is increased" (Hebb 1949, 62). His studies of the sequential firing of one neuron influencing another through contingency and contiguity became known as Hebbian learning. The mantra became popularized through a pivotal paper by Carla Shatz published in *Scientific America* in 1992 titled "The Developing Brain": "In a sense then cells that fire together wire together. The timing of action-potential activity is critical in determining which synaptic connections are strengthened and retained and which are weakened and eliminated" (Schatz 1992, 64). Understanding this correlation between neurons makes us recognize that the more one neuron communicates with another, the stronger the bond becomes between the two. This correlation is the process of associative learning, forging new connections through reinforcement. Where we focus strengthens those connections, and the memory of a particular action or thought becomes more prominent. This approach is fundamental when looking at patterns and sequences in our lives. When we infuse creative ways of enhancing our neural ability to develop a new way of completing a task, the synchronicity of one neuron firing with another builds a more robust network.

Learning through games, movement, and music are ways we can apply this associative learning style to developing healthy habits. Take exercise, for example. If the environment at the gym is not inviting and the music is not to our taste, it becomes hard to work out. However, if the music enlivens our spirit and lifts our mood, this reinforces our nervous system to align with the activity the body is doing at the time. Suppose we take this one step further and add a supportive class of fellow dancers or the setting of an outside hike; the happy networking of our brain fires away and reinforces these neural networks. This helpful workflow of internal communication reinforces the healthy activity and nourishment for your soul. Remember my tribe of Nia dancers? Their friendship and our rhythmic ritual of meeting to dance to music that moved our souls reinforced the positive health benefits of dancing for exercise.

This concept of pairing activities was the same strength I found for the workflows at the pharmacy. Sure, we could introduce technology and systems that would help prevent error—this was a crucial step. However, the human side of the equation was strongest when the individual felt supported and had created a pattern, a sequence, that reinforced the task. Find your support, pattern, and sequence that strengthens the outcome you are looking for, and you will see a natural shift in your ability to align with the tools needed to cultivate your potential.

Alignment also exists in the groups of individuals we choose to surround ourselves with as we journey through life. Are we choosing people that are positive and supportive? Is the content of what we digest on social media and the news feeding what we want to cultivate? Take time to reflect on your choices and recognize that you can say no to those who do not support your life path—you can turn off the content that derails you. Surrounding ourselves with family, friends, and communities that share our values encourages us to live authentically.

Authenticity is also essential in the workplace. Interactions that hold integrity and honesty feel grounded and real. Finding a work environment that is healthy and supportive feeds your well-being. Honor the desire to find work that you are passionate about, or if you bring presence, heart, and intention to the job you are doing, you may feel more satisfaction in your current career. Your contentment with work may also be related to work-life balance. If this equilibrium is present, the time you are working may not feel as difficult as for those whose scale is tipped in one direction. Aligning with meaningful and viable work may be all that is needed to feel at peace with your workplace.

The choices we make influence our path through life. How we feel about our choices impacts our state of well-being. To feel the flow of life's current as we dance with the people, events, and concepts we encounter provides us with the ability to stay connected within ourselves while we journey through the unknown. Opening and accepting the unfolding of events as they arise in life helps us hear the subtle internal messages as our path unfolds.

Finding the Path

There are times when we see a destination, a goal, or an outcome that we want to achieve. During my time in the wilderness, I saw a juncture between the tree line and the ridge that intrigued me. How would I arrive at my destination? What were the obstacles in the way? This physical challenge took me back to the trailblazing of my teenage adventures in the wilderness during high school. There were times when our group would stand and look across the valley at our destination. It seemed outside our reach as young teenagers to make our way across the rugged terrain. The seasoned guides leading us through the wilderness taught us how to navigate the landscape. I was fortunate to attend a high school that valued the student's connection to the natural world. In our outdoor education program, we were taught how to forge paths for ourselves. The physical trails through the wilderness translated to emotional approaches through peer pressure and the spiritual path of connecting with one's purpose. These skills in navigating life proved helpful as I transitioned to college and beyond. Determining our direction and finding our path can be challenging not only on outdoor adventures but also in navigating daily life.

The tools we learned to utilize for navigation on those high school adventures were a compass and a topography map. We learned to read the terrain to pick the best route. We can envision these tools as metaphors when mapping our journey of personal growth and development. However, instead of a physical compass and map, we learn to rely on our internal compass and the terrain of our inner knowing. Identifying these tools takes some introspection, but the clarity will be pristine once you connect with your inner compass. How do we connect with these tools? Quieting our mind and discerning the "felt sense" within our soul guides us to a more profound internal knowing. Some call this "felt sense" intuition; others call it following your gut. When you connect with the sensation of knowing that rises from the caverns of your body, you have found this type of knowledge that guides your genuine authenticity and sincerity. Your brain is calm and quiet, the sense of knowing rises from your belly, and the direction you take is guided by the heart.

If we feel uncertain and unsure of the terrain ahead, we may need to start with a map. One activity to try for wagering through the unknown is to make yourself a life map. You can reflect on where you have been or on where you are going. There is often some linearity related to the sequence of events that have occurred or that you hope will happen. Life mapping is a beautiful reflective process to help contemplate the events that have unfolded over the years. When you draw deeper into the present and connect with your intuition, it's easier to map the life within. One approach to mapping our internal terrain has been developed by my teacher and friend Elizabeth Murray. In her book *Living Life in Full Bloom: 120 Daily Practices to Deepen Your Passion, Creativity & Relationships,* she leads readers through four paths: the gardener, the artist, the lover, and the spirit weaver. For each path, she offers daily practices to "deepen your passion, creativity, and relationships." At the end of the book, she takes the reader through the process of what she refers to as life mapping. Through the process, you discover your North Star. "The center triangle is your North Star—your heart compass. It is like the balancing point of a compass, the place that is true and steady no matter what. Like your truth, values, and morals, it's what you can return to. It can steer you when you are in new territory or need assurance to discern your way" (Murray 2014, 195).

Elizabeth's life mapping process pulls from your natural skills and talents, incorporates your passions, and reflects on what the world needs. The process of incorporating what is needed in the world into one's map is powerful. It can be easy to focus on what we are receiving from the world versus what we are contributing. Conversations of entitlement and other arenas of personal agenda can cloud our vision. However, if we take the time to look within and connect with how we can tend to the garden of the soul, we will also see how that wellspring, once filled, can pour forth in service. Filling this internal reservoir fills our reserve; it strengthens our ability to give to our community and participate in the dance of life.

How do you integrate the process of giving yourself to others in service with cultivating the seeds of personal growth? There are two thoughts I would like you to contemplate. One is the way the beauty of a flower blesses the beholder without having to do anything. It just lives out its full intention of blooming, providing nectar and pollen, and fading. The impact of the flower came from just being. We, too, can make an impact from the vibrancy of our being. When we live out our full intention, our nectar and pollen can nourish and regenerate others. The second thought to contemplate is the gift of giving. Our lives are spiritually fed and emotionally restored when we participate in the lives of others. We are part of an ecosystem, and when we awaken to the interplay between the internal and external aspects of life, our vision of who we are is humbled and expanded simultaneously.

Most of us are aware that we are just one human among billions. You may think your actions and presence are insignificant. What would happen if the entire human population were to have these same thoughts? We would have a disaster on our hands because of the apathy that ensues when our connection with purpose or significance is lost. It's essential to recognize that our path in life matters. The steps we take on this earth do make an impact. When we see our presence as significant, then we also see the presence of others as significant. The interconnectedness of humanity and the environment of both our internal and external landscapes is revealed in this meaningful understanding of our worth. How do we navigate valuing ourselves and finding merit in others when the social and political structures appear amiss? Finding our path in the sea of humanity feels daunting at times. We need to bolster this voyage with guides and a community that coalesce in a common purpose—to live life with intention. Our purpose is our core guide.

To have an internal guide, an internal North Star, as Elizabeth Murray refers to in her book *Living Life in Full Bloom,* helps us return to our center. Have you ever considered developing a personal mission statement? Consider the value it offers the company employees when there is a central theme to their course of actions and decisions. Even when the path is unclear, when we know what guides us, taking on the uncertain terrain and foraging our path comes naturally.

Melodies

"When I drum I can hear my heart beat
I feel excitement from my head to my feet
It takes away my pain and worry
I don't feel like I am in such a hurry.

When I am drumming I feel free
My troubles fly away from me
And in comes all the peace and love
My spirit soars just like a dove.

When I am drumming with my friends
I feel like we are family
And when we drum we sound like one
One heart, one soul, one mind."
-Sean Scheuering, age 12
From *The Art and Heart of Drum Circles* by Christine Stevens (Stevens 2003)

Before my vision fast, all the participants met in the teepee on our guides' property. We gathered around a drum built by their mentor and whose story drew us together in its presence. In our gathering, we drummed as "one heart, one soul, one mind," as Sean so eloquently stated in his poem. The drum has been an instrument of transportation to other realms at various junctures in my life. From the guided visualization accompanied with a specific drumming beat in a therapy session to the experience of playing my djembe drum covered and strung by an African djembe drummer, my memories are filled with warmth and wonder when it comes to music.

Have you ever been in a terrible mood, but when you suddenly heard your favorite song on the radio, you felt free as a bird? Music transforms our souls. As Sean shares, it makes our "spirit soar like a dove." When we connect to the sounds of the song, we can pivot our mood. One day while I was in college, I was driving away from my friend's house, and she asked, "What are you listening to?" "Some headbanging heavy metal," I stated. "You need to be listening to something more uplifting," she replied. She proceeded to reach into my car, take out the CD I was listening to, and changed it to some upbeat reggae music. Now my brain was hearing, "everything little thing is gonna be alright," with a beat that shifted my foul mood to one of levity. But, of course, it's not always this easy. The next time you're feeling down or angry, try an experiment. Instead of choosing music that feeds your melancholy or feisty mood, try shifting it with a new tune. Take note of what happens.

The dance of synchronicity is about paying attention. If we set goals that we are disconnected from or force results that do not come to fruition, we feel defeated. What if we open the shutters and doors of our hearts and see what passes by? We can invite the stranger in for a cup of tea, see what they want to share, and let the dance of synchronicity begin. You do not have to have a house full of loud and obnoxious people. You can ask them to leave if their presence is straining. However, what happens is that you begin to attract people, ideas, and possibilities that bring you joy. Hang on to this idea, as these synchronicities may be just what you need when you are ready to grow.

Do you remember those embarrassing junior high dances? When I was in junior high, we had social events where we would gather to eat cookies and drink soda while a DJ spun our favorite tunes. The idea was to mingle and dance with each other. I had a blast when we all just jumped on the dance floor and boogied our hearts out. The embarrassing part was when the dreaded slow song came on, and we were expected to dance with a partner. Some kids naturally connected, and they enjoyed this part of the experience. I just waited until we could all go crazy on the dance floor in one big group. What I was missing was the chance to connect individually with another. I wanted to just groove with the masses. What would happen if I chose to just dance with one? Would there be any harm in trying to spend time with someone I didn't know?

Opening ourselves to unfamiliar people and the potential of chance meetings allows the dance of life to unfold. We connect with people of various backgrounds and different ways of approaching life. Having your viewpoint challenged can be a blessing. The people we thought we would never spend time with may have something of significance to add to our lives, and the flyer that flew in our face may have a message we are meant to read. The metaphorical dance is about living in the flowing current and inviting others to join us. It's about seeing and sensing flow in others and joining them. It's a dance because it's not static. There is an ebb and flow to this synchronicity that connects us in ways that we would never experience if we left the shutters and doors of our hearts closed.

Michael Singer does a fabulous job of sharing how he began to let life live him in *The Surrender Experiment.* He made deep connections and discovered profound insights. He lived his potentiality to its fullest by dancing this dance of synchronicity. He is the flower that is open and allowing the nectar that comes from within to nourish the lives of others. He went from wanting to be fully isolated and alone in his meditations to living the life of a teacher, author, and public figure. "By that stage of my growth, I could see that the practice of surrender was actually done in two, very distinct steps: first, you let go of the personal reactions of like and dislike that form inside your mind and heart; and second, with the resultant sense of clarity, you simply look to see what is being asked of you by the situation unfolding in front of you" (Singer 2015, 65).

When we step into this type of surrender, the dance begins, and we recognize that music comes in different forms. There is the melody of nature, the calm sound of a fountain, the composed piece, and the reassuring resonsnace of a friend's voice. Find the form that moves you; if you are uncertain, experiment. I have invited music into my life through singing, drumming, and playing the harmonium. I am not highly proficient at any of these musical mediums. It has been the exploration of sound and vibration that has moved me. Someday, when the timing is right, I will return to my musical practice. For now, plugging into what feeds my soul and shifts my mood is the melody I am currently cultivating. What small melody can you create, cultivate, and celebrate in your life?

To bring you closer to the healing power of music, I want to share a story with you from my friend David. David is a licensed pharmacist, but his passion is music. From building beautiful guitars from scratch to sharing his musical talent by playing at my wedding, I have seen David's ability to bring his inner harmony to life. He also plays music for patients at the hospital and has witnessed its healing power. Below is an excerpt from a piece that he wrote regarding his path to music therapy. To read the whole story, see Appendix B.

> *My true calling was revealed to me when my young daughter-in-law, Becca, was diagnosed with cancer. While in the hospital, I spent many hours playing for her. One day, a lady came in with a harp and asked Becca if she would like to hear some calming music. I was absolutely mesmerized by the session. She noticed my guitar*

case, and we ended up having a wonderful conversation about her work at the hospital. She mentioned that they were looking for another musician, specifically a guitarist, and asked that I consider joining. I didn't hesitate to say yes because I genuinely felt called and knew in my heart that I needed to be part of this community.

The only requirement was that I participate in an accredited program in clinical music. Throughout the course, I learned that this was not just about playing music, but it was also about gaining a scientific knowledge of sound and how it aids the healing process.

Stop and say the word "sound" and think about it. What do you hear? What comes to mind? Is it something pleasant? Something annoying? Sound is a vibration. We not only hear sound, but we can feel it as well. Just as we can feel the vibrations of a large truck as it passes by, our body feels the vibrations of music. Sound penetrates and has physiological effects on us, affecting our blood pressure, heart, and respiration rates. Our physical response is rooted in the brain. We are born with the ability to respond to music both physically and emotionally. Our hearing is one of the first senses that comes into play and one of the last to leave us. Studies have shown that we are able to hear in our mother's womb just as we have the ability to hear underwater. It is also the sense that continues working even if we are unconscious. It's measurable.

We can also make melodies with others in the community. As we align and connect with others who affirm and celebrate life, the music of our soul increases in volume. My solo becomes a chorus, and the potential for my message to be heard is amplified. I experienced this sensation of amplification when participating in a 5Rhythms dance retreat at Esalen. My dance was the "dance of many," as I explored the various stages of Gabrielle Roth's medicine mandala on the dance floor. In her book *Maps to Ecstasy: A Healing Journey for the Untamed Spirit,* Gabrielle Roth states: "Movement isn't only meditation; it's also medicine that heals the split between our minds and hearts, body and soul" (Roth 1998, 2). One of my dearest friends and I slipped into the signature 5Rythms patterns. Each of these rhythms represents what Gabrille Roth refers to as a different life stage, emotion, way of being, and aspect of self. Dancing had a transformational effect on her life and continues to influence the lives of others: "Ecstatic dance became a way of jumping out of my personality into my soul. Whenever I got stuck in my head, I did whatever it took to get dancing, to escape the safe, boring confines of being reasonable. I had no idea that I would spend my life taking others with me" (Roth 1998, 12). Dancing with Gabrielle on the cliffs of Big Sur took me beyond my physical and emotional limits. The sweat was dripping from my brow, and my clothes were soaked from the exuberance of the dance. I stood and felt healed from the integration of body, mind, and spirit. What are the rhythms you are dancing to in your life?

I am dancing in my soul, my heart, and my body as I write this to you. Somehow, somewhere, the synchronicity of finding the music that is the soundtrack to this book has met me, and I am pulsing with the energy of the ideas and concepts appearing on these pages. Align with what matters to you (create), build your community through connections on your path (cultivate), and sing out in celebration (celebrate). Find the beat that motivates you to keep moving forward and foraging your path in this life.

The Dance of Synchronicity Meditation

You stand firm and tall on your own two feet. The energy from the earth surges up into your legs, awakening nerves, muscles, tendons, bones.
It starts with a gentle sway, and then your shoulders begin to roll in their sockets. Finally, the juices of aliveness begin to flood your body.
Rhythms, beats, sensations pulse through your being. Your body dances you.
The direction of your dance is clear because it is arriving moment after moment. The melody of your soul provides the music.
The beat of your internal drum aligns you with your authentic self.
As you find your path through space and time, your connection within deepens. You expand and contract to feel the internal and external dimensions of your environment.
Your breath pairs with the movement, and a seamless unfolding of rhythm flows from your being.
The music slows, and the sweet nuance of stillness arises.

There is a place that opens itself to the sky and breathes in the fresh winds. It is a place where the past is forgotten and the present is found.

The grass and wildflowers here are surrounded by a forest of trees that secretly stand witness to the transformations that unfold.

It is a place where there is room to start a fire and see the thoughts and habits that no longer serve the individual or their community dissolve and float into the ether as dust carried by the wind.

All the elements needed are present, and the heart can find rest in this sweet bed of the earth.

Chapter 5

THE CLEARING

I left the cocoon of my solo spot, ventured across the babbling brook, and made my way to the clearing. The flat land and wide-open space felt stark compared to my place of retreat on the hillside among the trees. The journey to this spot was intentional. While preparing for the journey, I had considered the layers of my personality. There were aspects of myself I was willing to show, and there were aspects I felt I needed to mask to protect my more vulnerable attributes. The task at hand was to take off the masks and let them go. Sometimes the act of letting go is subtle and occurs over the course of time. At other times it calls for drastic action. The ritual of shedding my masks would be powerful. So powerful that I do not remember the masks; they have left me, and I am living from my wholeness.

Prior to my journey to the clearing, I had placed the physical masks I'd made for this time of introspection in the rough opening of an old tree stump. It was a cauldron working its magic on the layers of persona and the burdens of my heart. Why was I so set on holding on to these stories? What purpose did these façades serve? I reflected on these questions and realized they were layers of protection. I had grown accustomed to and comfortable with certain ways of being.

Knowing that fire precautions were essential, I needed a safe place for what was next. This is why I had ventured to the clearing. Here, out in the open, there were campsites with proper fire rings. I took my matches and the physical masks I had painted to represent attributes I was ready to release to the fire ring. This ceremony was the crux of transfiguration and the process of letting these layers dissolve. I struck the first fire safety match, and the sulfur smell filled the air as I held it to the papier-mâché and watched the cellulose fibers of the mask ignite into flame. The transformational power of fire is poignant.

As I witnessed the first mask disintegrate into ashes, I felt a sense of relief. I realized I no longer needed to carry the burden of the woundings associated with the past. My growth was possible; just as the tree grows and moves beyond fires and droughts, it was humanly feasible to move on. I proceeded to ignite the other two masks and watched their essence swirl up into the smoke and dissipate. When all that was left was a dusty grey heap, I felt complete. Nothing was lost; only a greater sense of self remained. I sat on the bumpy log near the edge of the smoldering fire and reflected on everything I had let go.

Letting Go

The process of burning the masks sparked a memory of a similar fire ritual I had participated in years before. It was along the shoreline with a close and dear friend. She supported me in doing something I had never done before: burn all my journals, heaps of them. We hauled wooden flats, bags of journals, and a box of matches to our spot. It was a large concrete fire pit in the sand. My friend inquired if this was what I seriously wanted to do. I responded with an emphatic yes. The words in the journals no longer served me and only reminded me of past pain and challenge. I was ready to let go of those words and the experiences and be freed from the weight of the journals. Our bonfire began. We didn't need kindling as the paper of the journals caught fire, and the ash danced in the flames. My heart danced along, and I felt the joy of releasing, freeing the words into the night air.

Letting go is a process. Sometimes it happens quickly, like a fire burning in the night, and other times, it can be a slow movement through the burdens that weigh us down. As we dive deeper into what it means to shed these layers, I want you to consider: What masks do you wear? And how does your desire to stay comfortable hold you back?

One method to create a significant metamorphosis and teach us profound lessons in the art of letting go is simplifying. Decluttering has become a movement with books like *The Life-Changing Magic of Tidying Up: The Japanese Art of Decluttering and Organizing* by Marie Kondo that teach us to only hold on to items that spark joy. What brought her to use this criterion was a voice that told her, "Look more closely at what is there" (Kondo 2014, 40). She recognized that this was the key to letting go "Because we should be choosing what we want to keep, not what we want to get rid of" (Kondo 2014, 41). We can take a similar approach to removing the junk from the drawers and closets in our hearts and minds. As thoughts filter (or flood) into our minds, we can hold them, examine them, and ask ourselves: "Does this bring me joy?" Why are we stuffing all these unwanted Post-it Notes and scribblings into the already crowded crevices of our minds? Let them go! Marie encourages people to toss, recycle, give away with absolute abandon. You can do the same thing with the mental noise that keeps you from your clarity.

Another resource that has supported my decluttering process is Courtney Carver's website and community, Be More with Less. I learned that Courtney had written books and taken various steps to launch her ideas into the world. Health issues are what prompted her shift, and she was able to find a true work-life balance. Her message of simplicity resonated with me. Courtney lives her message and connects with people through the act of simplifying. The beauty that results is not only a cleaner countertop but a deeper connection with personal clarity. The type of clarity that comes from being free from clutter is a mind that can see its path, dance with the synchronicities that arise, and flow with the current. Just as Marie Kondo connected with only keeping that which sparks joy, Courtney recognized that refining all aspects of life—body, mind, and spirit—brought a level of contentment inaccessible amongst the clutter and noise of our typical lives. She reflects on this in her book *Soulful Simplicity: How Living with Less Can Lead to so Much More*: "Once I began to identify what mattered to me and was doing what was necessary to protect it, I moved from frantic victim of busyness to gentle warrior. My tactics were fierce but also soft in defending my time from a society that always wants more" (Carver 2017, 146). I wanted to learn more about how to become this gentle warrior, so I joined Courtney's online community. At first, I felt lost and was unsure how to proceed. Then, during a live call, I listened to her talk, and she explained how to navigate the space. I was making it harder than it was. But, again, simplicity was the key.

Decluttering our minds of unneeded thoughts and removing the masks that no longer serve us takes us deeper. Like explorers, we engage our curiosity and investigate the roles that layering and protecting our thoughts and possessions play in our lives. Are these ideas and items in alignment with who we are? Do they serve our greater purpose? When we investigate further to understand why we are holding on to the masks and the clutter, we discover our resistance to being authentic and living a fully engaged life.

Dissolving Resistance

Meditation in the wilderness came easy. Being alone removed the distraction of conversation. Work, relationships, and errands were all saved for my return. The shedding of responsibility allowed me to attune to myself. In the forest, my only possessions were what I carried in my pack. The Internet, cell phone, and clock were not present. The lack of these distractions freed me to roam without the worries of time, people, or place. It was a taste of heaven on earth. I wanted to learn how to bring this same sense of freedom from external pressures into my daily life once I returned home from the woods.

Straddling the realms of spiritual life and the physical world can seem daunting at times. The construct of this duality stems from our perceptions that body, mind, and spirit are separate entities. When we blur the lines, we arrive at an unexpected clarity. The aspects of our lives do not need to fit into boxes, buildings, or boardrooms. The generosity of spirit that rises from a well-lived life flows from within and feeds the channels of family, friends, and coworkers. Our resistance must dissolve to allow the wellspring to rise and move freely through the layers of life. How do we dissolve resistance and find clarity? One modality that paves this path is meditation.

The most challenging meditation retreat I experienced was a Vipassana retreat in North Fork, California. A friend of mine had invited me to explore ten days of meditation at no cost. Ten days of free food and lodging sounded like an excellent idea to initiate a six-month sabbatical from my pharmacist career. My intention for this time away from work was to establish a deeper connection with myself. In addition, I figured this immersion in meditation would be a good way to quiet my mind and begin the process of going inward.

Vipassana is a longstanding meditation technique that explores connecting with the body's physical sensations to promote self-observation and exploration. I was still relatively new to the concept of meditation taught from an Eastern tradition. My previous years of spiritual reflection were based in a Christian context. My resistance and challenges started the moment we arrived. I bristled when I was asked to hand over my car keys. What!? Why would I need to give them my keys? Where was I going to go? I would later find out.

The intention of the retreat was to learn peaceful, silent, non-reactive presence with others while focusing on meditation. For ten days, we did not use words, gestures, or eye contact to communicate. The practice heightened my sense of presence both within and in the community as I navigated through the shared space. Learning to take turns when getting food was a new experience. There was no rush, and even the process of buttering my toast became a meditation. I tapped into the sensations that fluctuated through my body and noticed the circulation of thought in my mind as the days slowly passed.

I found the meditation practice challenging, and aches arose in my body. I was granted permission to sit in a chair in the back of the room. My resistance was strong and contributed to my physical discomfort. The fight against the process and place became so significant I wanted to leave. Now I knew why they took my car keys! My aunt and uncle lived by this lake town, not far from the retreat center. I thought about how long it would take to walk to their home. We were in the wilderness, and even their cabin was far beyond reach. I decided to visit the monk and ask for guidance.

When it was my turn to sit down in front of the monk, our lead meditation teacher, I almost felt speechless. I had not uttered a word in days, and here was my chance to speak up and say all the things that were upsetting me about this process and how the retreat was not for me. A few words began to formulate, and I shared my discomfort with her. Her response has stuck with me ever since. With a focused effect, she stated, "This is the pattern of your life, is it not, to seek change and leave what is uncomfortable?" Bam! A bolt of energy struck through me. I was confronted with myself. This desire to escape was my pattern and a pattern I struggle with to this day. If I do not like something, I change it.

I was not letting life flow through me. I was trying to redirect the river. I would need to let go of my agenda and expectations and give myself permission to be okay with what was unfolding around me. I left the meeting with the monk disgruntled. How did she know this was the pattern of my life? Her words resounded in my mind like a gong or a mindfulness bell; I began to loosen up and settle into the flow and routines of the retreat. I focused on my meditative walks that allowed my body to relax and my mind to focus on each step through the natural terrain.

Today, dissolving resistance is more about negotiations with my four-year-old and navigating life in a multigenerational household. From morning coffee to dinner dishes, my tendency to want things to go my way rises and falls. When I hold my preferences firmly, the waters get choppy, and when I release and flow with the current, I find the household harmony I am yearning for in the moment. Living life in moment-to-moment awareness helps me to recognize when I am resisting the current. It's not that I let the waters sweep me away or lose the sense of my personhood; it's more about my presence and how I pay attention to what is before me. How do you find presence in the tides of daily life?

Our breath is another powerful tool to connect us with the present moment. We can instantly slow our minds and reactions when we tap into the life-sustaining flow of air in and out of our lungs. Amazingly, something so accessible and inherent is often forgotten. Take a moment right now to stop reading and feel your breath breathing you. Feel its strength. Our breath is essential, yet we ignore it. Let the dialogue in your head fall to the background, hear the hum, and feel the vibration of your breath—its essence is essential, and focusing on its flow is a surefire way to experience the present moment. Connecting with our breath connects us with our body, our humanity, and how truly fragile life is.

The strength of our bonds to each other and the things we are drawn to in life can influence whether we find ease or struggle with letting go. The strength of these bonds impacts our ability to dissolve the resistance that holds us back from finding our contentment. In psychology, various modes of attachment relate to our upbringing and influence our security in relationships. What are the simple energetic bonds, the affinities we have to people, places, and things? I now recognize that letting go and dissolving resistance is a daily practice, a way of living. Sure, there are some things that I can release and allow to float down the stream. However, there are other aspects of liberating my life that are a part of my ongoing cultivation of a content and peaceful way of living.

How do we monitor our level of attachment in our daily activities? We are constantly generating new ideas, actions, and creations throughout life. The generative process is often more valuable than the outcome. It is through the acts of creating, planning, detaching, and cultivating that we grow. With keen attention and a loose grip, the continual evolution of our lives teaches us about the natural ebb and flow of thoughts, activities, and interactions. Our awareness brings insight into what holds us back and impedes our progression. Consider your flow through the waters of life. Are you grasping at branches to keep you in place or swimming freely?

Creative Expression

One tool that teaches the value of immersing yourself in generative action over arriving at the product is process art. I first learned not to be attached to what I make or create when attending high school. My art teacher wanted me to understand that creating was the most critical part of my artistic expression. This understanding is true for our personal development as well. The process of setting and moving toward a goal teaches us more than arriving at the goal itself. When I had spent hours molding and crafting a ceramic piece that exploded in the kiln, I had to put this concept into practice. How often do projects that we have spent hours investing in backfire on us? Do we crumble under the unexpected outcome, or do we rebuild? How do we strengthen our learning and growth? We can recreate with even more masterful skills by connecting to our process and holding awareness of what we learned. That day, I created a whole new piece from the shards that survived and saw the transformation that arises when we rebuild and reshape what we thought we were bringing into form.

I revisited this concept of process art when I took classes in expressive arts. What is expressive art? As defined by the International Expressive Arts Therapy Association (IEATA), "The expressive arts combine the visual arts, movement, drama, music, writing and other creative processes to foster deep personal growth and community development" (IEATA 2021). I dove deeper into using art as a means of personal exploration through classes with my dear friend and life guide, Christina Brittain. In classes like The Moving Brush, I saw how movement, painting, and personal exploration could meld into a healing experience. Her studio, The Art of You, was a palace of found objects, colors, and cozy corners. From the welcoming tea to the shelves of objects for the sand trays, I was in heaven. I wanted to live in the studio. I spent hours creating lighted-up trees from tumbleweed hot glued to a breadboard, painting my heart out on huge pieces of paper taped to the windows, and poring through magazines for the images I wanted for a collage that would reflect my heart's desires. In working with Christina in one-on-one sessions, classes, and book clubs, I have learned that honoring our authentic experience of life is how we begin to pull apart the layers of life to seek a greater connection with ourselves and our communities.

When we pull things apart, get curious about what's inside, and let go of the baggage that holds us back, the magic held in our seeds of potentiality sparkles. The resonance of the joy and simplicity we learned of in letting go becomes the catalyst for dissolving resistance. In releasing, refining, and rediscovering the bliss of keeping it simple, we return to joy. This poem, an excerpt from Christina's enchanting coloring book, reminds us…

<u>Joy is the Point</u>
Of course you want to enjoy your life!
You just keep forgetting to?
Here's your reminder:
Joy is still right here, right now!
Get back into the habit of happily discovering everything!
The thrill of a swing set.
A dandelion. Grass, Stars.
Laughter and squeals of delight are coming from your own heart,
and have been all along!
Remember!
You ARE joy.
Life is shining.
Turn your wild child face up to the sun and grin, grin again!
(Brittain 2016)

The power of authentic expression I connected with through the art-making process in Christina's magical studio continued in my coursework with Jane Goldberg when participating in her expressive arts training. I learned that dancing, singing, writing, and creating can cultivate healing in our lives that runs deep into the roots of our being. Jane said this beautifully in an interview: "All therapy is about learning to love yourself and others and expressing that love authentically out in the world. It doesn't matter if you sing it, paint it, dance it, write it or speak it out loud. Expressive arts therapy is an amazing opportunity to express creatively all that you are and, by doing so, to appreciate and acknowledge the main dimension of your being—your heart, mind, body, and spirit" (Ryan 2016, 22). There was no need for the expressions of the self to result in a painting to hang on the wall or a play to produce for Broadway. These creative explorations allowed the soul to surface and heal wounds. I have continued to find the value of processing life through expressive art. It's a process of living and letting go—it's a salve that soothes the spirit.

Living with a four-year-old has taken my level of understanding nonattachment to a whole new level. My son and I make a lot of collaborative art. It's a wonderful experience and teaches both of us how to be present and flow with each other. There are times when I love what I see emerging on the paper, the cement, the sand, or even in the three-dimensional structures we have built. The impermanence of the form produced helps me recognize that everything we are creating is part of life's natural ebb and flow. The vivid display of colored chalk on the cement outside fades with the rain or the water from the garden hose. The tides of the ocean eat the sandcastles. And the fervor of a four-year-old can crumple a masterpiece in a matter of seconds. What I have come to appreciate is that we are creating for the sake of creating—nothing else.

Releasing expectations of what we produce allows us the freedom to be fully present in our process. The words flow freely, the movements unfold naturally, the paint moves over the paper with ease. We can apply these same concepts to how we approach daily life. The budget, house, or work project can become tedious when we are consumed with the outcome. When we recognize that the outer layers can break down, they are meant to break down because the potential is in the core of the seed. We can let the processes of our lives happen naturally, more organically, with ease. Solutions will arise just as the seed produces the sprout. Dissolving resistance allows us to arrive in the process of living life.

Arriving

I often find myself living in another time and place—in my mind. My desire for something different keeps me from this present moment. I think of the next job, a different place to live, and yearn for new circumstances in my life. I transport myself to the future, or I float back in time, ruminating on what had been and wondering what would have happened if life had taken a different turn in the stream. This time travel prevents me from seeing the beauty and awe of the life unfolding in front of my eyes. While on my vision fast, my "vision" was seeing the value of inhabiting each moment of life. This deep presence was the practice of living a full and vibrant existence. To arrive fully present, we must be alert to where our attention rests. Arriving. Here. In this moment. Opening my eyes to the reality and serenity of what is allows me to experience a deepening, a rooting in, that brings presence and peace.

To recognize the significance of who we are—rather than what we have, where we live, or when we will achieve the next goal—is profound. The constant in the equation of our lives is ourselves. Regardless of any situational factor or outside influence, you are always you. When we conceptualize that we are a huge mass of cells and atoms moving through space and time, it allows us to be in awe and acceptance of our humanity. Do you know who taught me this? My precious son and his four-year-old inquisitiveness. Let us get curious. What happens when we allow our cells to do what they naturally do? When we live in the present moment, stress melts.

Pause to notice the sounds, sights, and smells of your everyday experience. Engage your senses. This pause will automatically pivot your perspective.

Our seeds of potentiality do not need material acquisitions, certificates, or the approval of others. All they need is nutrient-rich soil, water, and sunlight. They need to be planted. Planted inside of us so their roots can grow, and their shoots can unfurl. How do we tend to the gardens that are our lives? Here is a simple experiment with real seeds that speaks volumes. We took four cups, three filled with soil and one with sand, and planted seeds so we could see how they fared under different circumstances. The seeds in one of the cups were denied water, and the seeds did not grow at all. The seeds in the cup that were sheltered from the sunlight grew and then quickly faded. The seeds in the cup that were planted in the sand grew but struggled as small plants that lacked nutrients. Finally, the seeds in the cup that received all three—sunlight, water, and good soil—flourished. How do we translate this experiment into our lives? Let us consider how we flourish.

Flourishing

Flourishing comes from providing these core ingredients of nourishment in our lives—water, soil, and sunlight. What are the equivalent elements in our humanity? This contemplation is a profound question with volumes written by philosophers, psychologists, physicians, and others looking to categorize essential human needs. To distill the wisdom into something attainable and pertinent to your life, let's discover the attributes that provide **you** with the physical, emotional, and spiritual components of water, soil, and sunlight. We are told what we need by others—parents, spouses, friends, the media—anyone or anything outside of us. Do you need to be told? Or do you already know what calls from within to feed your soul? When the answers come from our innate wisdom, we do not forget. They may get buried under piles of external expectations and ideas, but if we clear the rubbish and connect with the essence of who we are, the elements that truly nourish us are revealed.

Obtaining water. Let us connect with our inner chemist for a minute. Think about a glass of water. At the top, there is a layer of water molecules bonded together with a stronger force than the other molecules in the glass. This chemistry is referred to as surface tension. When you drink that water, you break and dissolve those bonds, and the water moves freely. Breaking through the surface tensions of your life can be just as easy. The molecules of life act in accordance with the concepts of chemistry. Take a sip. Move through the tension and break the bonds. Let your soul quench its thirst.

Accessing the sunlight. The love and light that are at the threshold of our existence are waiting to come in. They are knocking. Will we open the door? Will we let the light in through the windows? Maybe we can at least peek. There are people standing there offering to share their light. Open. Receive. Accept. If we feel alone, it's so much harder. We are not alone. We are connected. We only perceive that we are isolated. The threads of life connect us with so many individuals. And if we shift our focus, we see a web of support surrounding us, breathing with us, communicating with us, and cheering us on.

Choosing nourishment. There were times while on the trails during my vision fast when my pack felt heavy, and I wondered why I chose to burden myself by bringing too much "stuff" with me. The weight and burden of what I carried made the inclines so much harder. However, when I turned my attention to the beauty that surrounded me and the companionship that had carried me to that point, my situation felt lighter. Do you weigh yourself down with "stuff," or are you choosing the nourishment of life-giving relationships and connections with the natural world around you?

To access the elements, you need to grow, allow yourself to be broken. When the surface tension breaks, when the outer structures of our lives crumble, the water and light will come through the cracks. The concept of inhabiting a solid structure is simply a mental construct. You are whole. All the pieces of you make up the whole. And you are interconnected with the environment around you. The water, light, and nourishment our seeds of potentiality need come from the symbiosis of living in tune with the world around us. Instead of isolating in fear, connect with the whole of life.

Where is my mountain lion!? I am ready to roar with her. The energy of the lioness, the internal fire, or the motivational urge to change gives rise to the kinetic potential to overcome the energy barrier of moving forward. All this amazing potential energy is packed into seeds—the seeds of potentiality. The seed releases its protective covering by sending roots deep and emerges through the topsoil by pushing through the resistance. There is no shortcut. The resistance dissolves as we move through the tensions and grow past the challenges. In this life cycle of growth, we continue to arrive in the present moment and stand in the beauty of life.

The Clearing Meditation

You are sitting on the earth in meditation, following the inflow of your breath.
You see a pool of water, and you peer into the reflective surface. It's a mirror that shows you an image of your face and the façades that you project. You are stunned by this piercing reflection of yourself, and you take a moment to reconnect with your breath and ground into the strength of the earth that supports you.
At first, it seems that it's only a reflection ... then your true authentic self lifts through the façades floating on the surface of the water and rises above.
The masks hover at the surface, and when you try to retrieve them, you realize they are dripping with the burdens they hold.
You understand that seeing these masks so clearly is a gift—a gift from your true essence.
You lift the masks from the water and place them in a brittle tree stump. As they dry, you contemplate the role they have served in your life. You discover these masks no longer serve you. You are ready to let them go.
To dissolve their presence, you stand up and retrieve them from the stump. A magical transformation has begun to take place, and you are prepared to take the next steps.
As you stand between the reflective pool and the tree stump, you look out in the distance. There beyond the trees, you see a clearing. Slowly you walk toward this opening where the spaces between the trees let the light stream into the forest of your heart.
There is a sweet aroma in the air, one of the wildflowers drifting through the atmosphere. You feel the call to this next step and walk into the clearing. There you find a fire ring circled by beautiful rocks and stones. There is a box of matches and a glass of water.
You strike the match and set the first mask aflame. The brilliant blues, oranges, and yellows of the flame mesmerize you. You set

the burning mask in the fire pit and watch it disintegrate into ash.
You take the next mask and the next.
You repeat this process until all the masks have vanished.
You feel complete.
You take a sip of the amazingly cold water and then smother the remaining fire. The swirl of the smoke rises and fades. You take a moment to feel the lightness in your heart. You have dissolved the resistance by letting go of what was holding you back. You have arrived. Arrived at the truest sense of yourself.
As you begin to leave the clearing, you see a sweet blanket of wildflowers among the grass. You gently lay your body on the nurturing earthen floor among the wildflowers and slip into a sweet rest.
This state of contentment is your new home.
It is not a place, an idea, or a concept that lives outside of your body.
It is you.

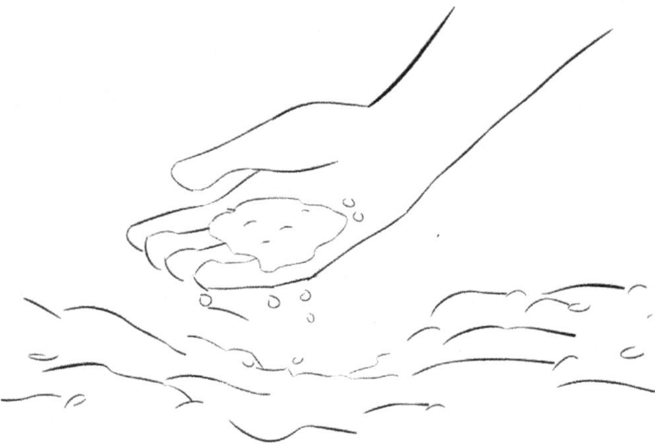

There is a deep rich place in the soil of life that carries the nutrients needed for creation. The sustenance provided allows for the vital processes of growth.
The way the soil is enriched influences the quality of the growth that takes place in its presence. When it is sifted through with the touch of care and attention, the soil breathes in the air and is renewed, ready for another cycle. When cultivated with love, it provides the perfect home for potential to be planted.

Chapter 6

THE TURNING OF THE SOIL

The sensual stimulation of the natural world was like a warm blanket that held me safe and secure as I dug deep into my inner terrain. Nestling into the protruding roots of the grandmother tree, I became entranced with their intricacy. The sheer mass of the roots was impressive as they crept over rocks and anchored deep into the earth. She was unlike any other tree I could remember, and I wondered what made her so unique. Some of the exposed roots were worn smooth, and others were craggy as they sprawled out beneath her magnificent crown. She was regal, yet her wisdom was tangible in the sturdiness of her trunk and roots. As I think back to this moment, my heartstrings are tugged, and I yearn to crawl into the arms of the grandmother tree—to feel her hold and reassurance.

In reflecting back to our first task of selecting our solo spots for the four days and four nights of our vision fast, I could now see the importance of my site for this time of turning my inner soil. When seeking out my place of solitude, ideas of the perfect cocoon for my metamorphosis danced in my head. I envisioned finding a spot with just the right elements to nurture my internal transformation. Clambering up rocks to look for hilltop clearings and seeking in the crevices of the hillside for tucked-away retreats, we realized this task was more challenging than we anticipated. Finding sites with access to water and flat, suitable areas for sleeping seemed to be at a minimum. Sometimes finding our spot in life can be just as challenging.

Digging Deep

My vision fast was a time of introspection while being immersed in the stunning beauty of the wilderness that surrounded me, including the grandmother tree. We often find reassurance in the physical structures of life. Whether it's the warmth of a hug from a friend or the comfort of our homes, our sense of touch and the feeling of containment grounds us. The roots, trunk, and branches of the grandmother tree are the physical structures that contain her wisdom, her energy, and her spirit. Our bodies are the physical structures that hold the inner workings of our humanity, the deep and hidden parts. The complex network of neurons, signaling systems, organs, muscles, and bones is your physical root system. Each complex human system holds significance in sustaining our livelihood. Our emotional and spiritual lives are integrated with the root system of our physical framework. The mapping of these systems reveals the intricacy of the interwoven network that lives beneath the surface of our skin.

Understanding the organization, connections, and relationships of the layers of our lives helps us to develop the stewardship of our humanity. How we care for our physical, emotional, and spiritual systems is vital to cultivating the garden of our lives. So how do you dig deep and inspect the inner workings of your body, mind, and spirit?

One tool for digging deep is curiosity. The inquisitiveness of my son reminds me to be fascinated with the concept of investigating the inner workings of just about anything. From how the sink drains the water to how our body works, he wants to dive deep and understand the way things work. He and I have been reading David Macaulay's books to further his exploration of science and the human body. The author recognizes our familiarity with our external world over the internal. "Because it works twenty-four hours a day, seven days a week, and makes only a few routine demands on our schedules, it's hardly surprising that we're much more familiar with its outside appearance than we are with what's going on inside" (Macaulay 1988, 9). Macaulay's drawings take you into this inner world and explore the details of how our bodies work.

From the cells we started as to the complex multicellular systems that constitute our physical bodies, his portrayal is both realistic and imaginative. This description inspired my son's drawings and three-dimensional building and reflected the concept of the "blow-up" image that zooms in and looks at the next level of detail. I was just ushered into his room to see a drawing of a vein focused on a zoomed-in detail of a red blood cell and a white blood cell. The deeper detail provides insight into the microscopic level of life that may not be apparent at a quick glance.

We can do this same type of "zooming in" and "blowing up" the details in our introspection. For example, I always react with a short temper when asked about my schedule. Why? Zoom in on schedule—what comes up? The feeling that I don't have enough time to do the things I need to do and want to do. Ah-ha! Zoom in further—exploring what I want to do feels stifled, and I'm overcome by what I need to do. Zoom in on "stifled" and explore what I'm not getting to do that wants to be expressed. Two things arise: More time for artistic expression and more time to declutter. Zooming in revealed that my short fuse was surfacing because I was not honoring a call from deep within. My creative soul wanted time and space to express itself through designing and maintaining a beautiful space to live. Through my introspection, I more clearly saw my story of lacking time and space. Attending to my physical space echoed the need to create emotional ease and breathing room in my daily operations of being a mom, wife, daughter, and budding author.

When we carry these deep internal stories, their influence affects our ability to live fully in the present. In exploring your seeds of potentiality, you have spent time releasing, allowing uncertainty, aligning with your values, and letting go. These processes create the space to cultivate our internal terrain. Just as a garden bed is cleared before planting a new crop or a beautiful display of flowers, the soil of our lives needs to be tended to for the seeds of potentiality to have the support required for growth. This humus of the earth is where a healthy root system can expand—just as our connection with the soil of our soul provides for our human flourishment.

You may be wondering, what is the soil of my soul? It's the energetic layers of body, mind, and spirit as they are held together by the fabric of life. The health of your physical tissues, mental state, and devotional self are all influencers of how the seeds we plant transcend their dormancy and bloom into the fullness of their potential. Are we in a fragile state, or are we filled with the fullness of life? If we feel broken when we are trying to love and support others, it may be time to look at our attentiveness to ourselves. The balance between self-care and service to others is important when considering the state of our internal soil. We need connection—connection with self and relationship with others.

Digging deep into the internal terrain of our lives can feel messy. So we put on our work clothes and don our gloves. This preparation for looking within is helpful because it tunes our mindset to the introspection at hand. When we dig beneath this rough topsoil that has withstood the storms of life, we see something simple and pure below—our authenticity. Under the rocks and rubble is a beautiful deeper layer of humus; it's the nutrient-rich layer that has resulted from the natural emotional composting of our lives. They mix when we allow the hurt, pain, joys, and celebrations of daily living to break down. The result of this mixture is your internal soil.

How do you dig deep, examine the soil of your soul, and integrate the inner aspects of yourself? You can investigate your internal soil through journaling, meditation, or self-inquiry. Approach the examination like a scientific gardener—get curious and dig in with your trowel and place your findings under the light of the microscope. As you turn the soil in your inquisition, you bring air and light to the internal terrain. The focus on the soil's microcosm may bring insight into what is occurring in the macrocosm of your life. This process gives the internal soil the aeration it needs, and you can inspect the contents. The turning of the soil allows anything stuck or clumped together like a dirt clod to be broken apart and mixed into the larger container of the bed. Then vital nutrients can be incorporated to bring balance and improve the quality of the soil. This process of breaking down and mixing is a part of the internal composting process that allows our experiences to incorporate and enrich our lives without creating tension or hardness. We are aiming for soft, supple, nutrient-rich soil—this is the desired soil for our seeds of potentiality.

How do we bring balance into our lives and improve the quality of our physical, emotional, and spiritual soil? One way is to connect with your creative spirit. As we talk about the metaphorical process of gardening, you may find yourself trying your hand at digging in the dirt of your yard or starting a container garden on your balcony. Fran Sorin wrote a wonderful book about the creative use of gardening in cultivating our lives. In her book titled *Digging Deep: Unearthing Your Creative Roots through Gardening*, she states, "My mission is to show new and experienced gardeners alike how they can use their gardens—be they rolling, manicured lawns or tiny blank plots of land—as tools for their creative awakening. I believe from the depths of my heart that gardening can be one of the profound ways to unearth the creative spirit buried in every one of us" (Sorin 2004, xiii). Your seeds of potentiality lie in your creative spirit. Let this be the bed, the soil that is cultivated and nurtured to manifest a life of beauty and abundance.

Gratitude

Another way to amend the soil of our souls for a well-nurtured garden is to develop the mindset of gratitude. Gratitude is a vital nutrient, just as nitrogen and phosphorus are needed to balance the soil. When we observe and take note of what we are thankful for, our appreciation has positive effects on the health of our bodies. Were you aware of the numerous advantages of a grateful heart? In addition to improved physical health and sleep patterns, saying thank you reduces your anger, increases your ability to empathize, and brings stability to your mental state. And since you will be a nicer person to be around, you will tend to generate more social connections; feeling connected will amplify your sense of well-being. When you feel better physically, emotionally, and socially, your self-perception improves. This generation of appreciation for who you are enhances your self-esteem. Improving your confidence builds your resilience. Are you ready for a cup of gratitude!?

Developing your sense of gratitude grows an appreciation for all aspects of life. The positivity generated will begin to flow from us through compliments, random acts of kindness, and happiness. The impact grows beyond our contentment and influences the lives of others. There are incredible resources to help cultivate gratitude in your life. You can find a list of these in the resource section of this book. I encourage you to try different approaches to see what resonates with you. It may be keeping your own gratitude journal, or you may find teaching children to have a mindset of appreciation builds your disposition of being grateful. One method that impacted my personal development of a gratitude practice was the work of Angeles Arrien.

Arrien's book *Living in Gratitude: Mastering the Art of Giving Thanks Every Day* provided the foundation for a weekly gathering of women in an online community. Arrien shares both the depth and far-reaching impact of this practice in the introduction of her book: "The expression of gratitude is essential to humankind's sustainability and survival. Gratitude's stabilizing and healing effects, which have been researched from multiple standpoints—cultural, psychological, physical, spiritual, even financial—have made it abundantly clear that the benefits of living a grateful life are irrefutable" (Arrien 2013, 2). Elizabeth Murray, the heartfelt teacher I introduced earlier, leads the group that focused on using watercolors as a means for meditating on our gratitude. We would gather found objects or venture into our gardens to find pieces of the world around us that reflected the messages of our hearts. We painted rosemary for remembrance, olive branches for peace, and roses for love. The influence of cultures and stories reminds me of our communal connections. This connection was especially touching during the holidays when we painted the angels and spirit guides from different spiritual beliefs and traditions. It was a circle of encouragement and introspection. Finding these groups in your community or the global community can feed your soul.

The groups and communities we connect with are our ecosystems. The garden of our lives is constantly connected with the world around it. When we turn the soil and dig deep, we recognize that the soil does not stand alone. The soil is a part of the larger system, the ecosystem of our existence. Taking the time for introspection helps us connect with meaning and significance. When we identify these vital components, our clarity on nourishing and feeding those parts of our lives comes into focus. What important part of your life needs attention and nourishment?

Nourishment

My rite of passage experienced through my vision fast was centered around the concept of fasting from food for four days and nights. Fasts have been used for thousands of years as part of spiritual rituals and in times of personal reflection. A rite of passage is an opportunity to step fully into your life and reclaim your wholeness. To understand what our health depends on, we need to see the components of what sustains and nourishes our body, mind, and spirit. The journey required vigor and stamina, yet on a more subtle level, it was a time to digest life's experiences and emerge with fresh eyes.

This renewed perspective helped me consider how I was nourishing myself physically, emotionally, and spiritually. Our level of nourishment impacts our health, vitality, and ability to cultivate our seeds of potentiality. Utilizing the metaphor of our personhood as the garden of our life, we can see the importance of the soil where these seeds are planted. If the soil is depleted, the seeds are missing some of the vital nutrients needed to grow. How we nourish ourselves is vital to our overall health and well-being.

The substances we supply to our body, mind, and soul influence many layers of our lives. Nutrition is a vital piece to our sustainment of good health. What we choose to eat affects our waistline and affects the inner workings of the cells within our body. We can influence these intricate systems by how we feed them. When I think about how the slice of chocolate cake with ice cream impacts my cells versus cacao chia seed pudding, I may pause and make my decision based upon health instead of desire. Do I live to eat or eat to live? The most important aspect of our nutrition is developing a healthy relationship with food. What I do know is that there is no one-size-fits-all remedy when it comes to diet. Learn about your body's specific needs, keep a food diary, notice which foods augment your energy and sense of well-being and which foods pull you down and leave you in dis-ease.

My good friend Liscia, a fabulous massage therapist, says the tissues of the body are like the soil of Mother Earth. She shares her reflections in her blog post, "Life as a Somatic Exploration," to further this point: "Structured in our body posture and moving through our energy system are the emotions and experiences of our life. Somatic (body) practices are awareness-oriented approaches that connect us with our bodies. If we recognize that... our attitudes, beliefs, values, hopes, dreams, fears, memories, and experiences are expressed through our body and reflected in the way we move through the world, then we realize it is possible to access greater understanding of ourselves through connecting with the body" (DiGiacomo 2021). We need to tend to our bodies just as we tend to our gardens. The turning of the soil in the garden allows the plants to find an inviting home to thrive. Massage breaks down the clots, melts tension, and welcomes nourishing endorphins. In addition, the movement created by massage improves circulation, allowing for improved blood and lymphatic flow throughout the body. When you consider all the fantastic health benefits of massage, it's easy to see how tending to this soil of your physical body is essential in cultivating your overall well-being.

When we consider the body's tissues, muscles, and bones, we tune in to how we are moving and taking care of them. From the osteoclasts that produce bone to the fibers that hold everything together, nutrition, exercise, and sleep all impact our body's ability to thrive. How do we motivate ourselves to tend to this vital garden within? Are we willing to offer ourselves the same level of loving care that we offer others? Be a creative scientist. Get curious and explore. Too often, we try to fit ourselves into a box, program, or app that does not work for us. Find what resonates and works for you. Be relentless. Your cells depend on you. They have the potential to regenerate and serve you; serve them!

It takes tending to your sleep, your thoughts, your mood—the wholeness of you—to tend to the soil of your body, mind, and soul. Another way we can thrive is to find methods of self-care that revive us. Do you feel rejuvenated by a cup of warm tea in the sunlight or a yoga session that connects you to your breath? Sleep and hydration are cornerstones to my ability to be present and inhabit my day. Find what you need by calling on your inner scientist. Before making any changes, first, study your life. Get curious about the patterns in your life. Observe what you are doing and record it. By knowing how you currently spend your time and how you feel while engaged in the various activities, you will begin to awaken to where shifting patterns and behaviors may be helpful. Grab a blank notebook and just jot down what you can. Tracking, reflecting, and journaling can be revealing and serve as a form of accountability. You are the expert on yourself, and by getting to know the ins and outs of your daily routines, you may find the answers to sustaining your health!

We have established that nourishment does not only consist of the food and water we feed our system, but it also entails how we feed our souls. Everything we take in through our senses affects our well-being. Our friends, both those we see and interact with and those who are virtual, can impact our perceptions of ourselves and the world around us. The news, the communities we live in, and the events in our country and the world can also influence us. By staying connected to ourselves, our authenticity, and what we value, we can filter or disengage from the information that does not enhance our lives.

Choose nourishment that is life-affirming for your body, mind, and soul. When I prepare a garden to be planted, I take time to prepare the soil. I turn the ground over and add organic nutrients to the exposed earthen material. Introspection is a beautiful method for turning the soil of our souls. In our process of digging deep, we connect with our inner terrain. Reflecting on what is missing and abundant in our lives helps us understand what is present, what needs to be added, and what might be out of balance. Just as the soil needs the right balance of nutrients, our lives need the right balance of love, healthy food, and clean air and water. Humanity needs this balance. Where do we find the resilience to build communities that feed all aspects of human life?

An experience that introduced me to the beauty of living with this level of intentionality was the time I spent at Mount Madonna Center in the Santa Cruz Mountains. I think of my time there when I think about nourishment because I lived in a place of self-care for three months while being dedicated to Karma Yoga (selfless action). Living in this community included yoga, meditation, service-based living, gardening, and a deeper connection with just being.

Baba Hari Dass was the sweet soul who inspired this intentional community. His commitment to silence taught others that outstanding leadership does not come from words or a loud presence. His gentle and soft demeanor provided greater guidance than motivational speeches or traditional thought-driven orchestration of people. If you are interested in learning more about his teachings, I suggest *Everyday Peace: Letters for Life.* He shares letters he has written to individuals regarding spiritual life, relationships, yoga practice, and more in this book. He shares in one letter, "A tree is inside a seed in subtle form. When the seed is sown, the tree comes out in the gross form. In the same way all knowledge is already in our mind and by doing yoga this knowledge comes out like a tree from a seed" (Hari Dass 2000, 109).

Daily rhythms were easy at Mount Madonna because they were decided for me. Mealtimes, yoga class, and times for service were predetermined, taking the pressure of decision-making off my shoulders. While I was free to flow with the daily currents of life in this community, I enjoyed the slower pace. There was room in my day to sit in the sun and drink in the beauty of the garden. I also wandered the extensive trails among the redwoods as a time of reflection and regeneration. Why have we lost this sense of ease and supported pace for life?

We can slow down and integrate the various layers of nourishment into our lives. Enjoying our human experience can be like making a fantastic cup of chai tea. It takes more time and intention than dipping a tea bag into a cup of boiling water. While at Mount Madonna, one of the most revered tasks was making chai for afternoon tea with Baba. And just like this tea, in life, the spice—the warmth and flavor—comes from our interactions with the people and places we encounter on our life journey. The strength of the tea depends on how long it's steeped in the boiling water. If we ruminate on our thoughts and let them steep too long, we can become bitter just as the tea turns too strong when left in the water too long. The milk adds a smooth velvety texture and feels synonymous with our self-care. Lastly, sugar needs to be enough to make the experience pleasurable and achieve just the right sweetness level.

How will you nourish your life? How will you prepare your cup of chai? By taking mindful steps to attend to your physical, emotional, and spiritual needs, you will amend the soil of your life in a way that will help cultivate your seeds of potentiality. Fasting helped me reevaluate what I was taking in and consider the actions needed to prepare my internal garden in a way that would support abundance and vitality. Once this soil has been turned and amended, it's ready for the seeds to be planted. Soon they will push their roots through and establish themselves in the well-nourished soil of our souls.

Being Planted

Identifying suitable terrain to plant our seeds of potentiality may feel daunting. Seeds need nutrient-rich soil to flourish. In our exploration of nourishment, we have examined how amending the soil provides the attributes needed for growth. Once the soil is prepared, there are additional measures to take into consideration. I recently planted seeds in our backyard garden with my son. To ensure success, we read through the instructions on the seed packets. Each seed type had specifics for how deep to plant the seed, appropriate spacing, temperature requirements, and sun exposure recommendations—taking in these directions for planting these seeds that would one day become vegetables clued me in to the importance of having the right parameters for our personal growth. If the elements are not conducive to introspection, communal connections, and self-care, then how can we expect to have the right environment for our potential to grow and unfold? When the soil of our life is strengthened and the conditions are maintained, the seeds we have planted have a greater potential to flourish.

Analyzing, strengthening, and choosing the right environment are vital steps in gardening because the plant cannot grow without the support and nourishment of the soil. There must be a physical place to grow. Although we are focused on our personal metaphysical growth, we must accept our humanity and recognize that all growth occurs in a physical vessel. How do we support this intertwined growth of body, mind, and soul? By establishing the soil of our lives as the container for our growth and the supportive sustenance for being planted.

Once we have inspected the soil and have decided it's a good spot for germination, we grow in confidence that we can now plant our seeds of potentiality. These seeds will need physical, emotional, and spiritual support. The soil in which the seeds are planted is the support system of the seed. Since our humanity consists of these physical, emotional, and spiritual layers, let us consider each of these attributes as aspects of the support system.

Physical support. Our seeds of potentiality need an internal terrain that will support their growth and expansion. When well-nourished and tended, the framework of our tissues and internal systems within our physical body provides this sustaining soil. The nutrients are carried by the water in our bodies throughout the passageways and are delivered to their most needed destinations. The significance of our hydration will become even more apparent when we experience the sunrise in the garden in an upcoming chapter. At that juncture, we will see how the interplay of soil, water, and sun coalesces. In addition to food and water, we also thrive on a good night of rest. Sleep is a time when our body recalibrates and attends to systems that need attention. Think about how sluggish our computers become when we leave them constantly running and neglect system updates. How can we expect these machines to keep up with us with cluttered desktops and overtaxed random-access memory (aka RAM)? Well, we overrun our bodies, and our memory gets foggy, and we need a reboot. Sleep is the time we can truly support this functionality of our bodies. When we tend to these physical needs, we are also tending to our emotional needs.

Emotional support. Through both connection to community and focusing on self-care, we tend to our emotional well-being. We will look at these support systems in more detail in the next chapter as the roots of our potential push through the encasing of the seed. At this time, I am taken back to the process of establishing my solo spot with my check-in partner. Looking for our spots together was an exercise in both connection and self-reflection. We settled on our two solo spots, which were near a location where we took daily pilgrimages and left creative rock arrangements to indicate that we were doing fine. This communication was our only link to another person during our time in solitude. The value of the check-in partner extends beyond my time in the wilderness. When we take on new challenges, it's helpful to have someone to provide encouragement and to be an accountability partner along the journey. There are also support groups that offer heartening connections for individuals faced with similar challenges. When we feel alone, the greatest act of personal care can be taking steps to connect with our community.

Spiritual support. How do we stay supported during times of introspection and spiritual growth? It may seem easier to live in the outside world at times, since digging deep and going within can be scary terrain. We may refrain from connecting within by allowing social media, the news, and our favorite television shows to distract us. Connecting with spiritual communities, encouraging books, or causes that carry us beyond our own perceived problems can shift an overemphasis on the self to a healthy incorporation with the world around us. This integration with our external ecosystem reminds us of our reverence for the earthen systems that support our existence.

One practice that incorporates all three layers can be found in the book *Earthing: The Most Important Health Discovery Ever!* by Clinton Ober, Stephen Sinatra, and Martin Zucker. Ober unveiled the electronegativity of the earth's surfaces and its direct relationship to our potential to heal. "If somebody is in direct contact with the earth—barefoot or through one of his grounding pads—the free electrons flow into the conductive circuitry of the body and snuff out inflammation. Inflammation causes pain. People with pain who are grounded experience less pain" (Obner 2010, 52). The practice of "earthing" entails taking off your socks and shoes and standing on the grass or soil. The earth is here supporting us day in and day out. By connecting the energy of your internal terrain to that of the earth, you will feel supported. This support flows through all systems and aspects of your body. You will feel connected to yourself and to the planet you stand on every day. The more we connect to the resources and energy provided by this amazing planet, the more we will connect with our role in the ecosystem of our existence. Being planted helps us slow down and recognize that when we are rooted in ourselves, our presence takes hold and grounds us.

One aspect of our support system that does not receive the attention it deserves is the poor quality of the earth's soil. Understanding the depletion of the physical soil our crops grow in today helps us understand the depletion of the metaphorical soil of our humanity. Learning how to improve the soils of our land will teach us about our growth. How? By showing us that overworking and overtaxing the earth diminishes the nutrients it holds. Kiss the Ground is a nonprofit organization that leads soil advocacy trainings and regenerative gardening courses. Their purpose is to "educate existing and emerging leaders about the solutions that lie within the soil and train them to be influential advocates in their homes, communities, and in their businesses to drive structural change toward regeneration through grassroots action" (Kiss the Ground 2021).

The sustenance of our survival is rooted in how we interact with the dirt of the earth and how we tend to the clay that is shaped into the lives we live. Our intentions toward ourselves and the environment in which we live are critical for this balance to be realized. Unfortunately, when our daily lives include grabbing food on the go, keeping busy with one activity after the next, and losing track of our true priorities, we forget to nourish ourselves. The time has come to establish a fortified bed of nourishment, both in our personal lives and for the creatures of the planet. We can then plant the seeds of potentiality you have identified in the well-nourished soil of your soul and see them thrive in an ecosystem that supports their growth. It's time for the roots to push through and the potential to burst into life.

The Turning of the Soil Meditation

You find yourself relaxing into the soft surface of the warm soil. It holds you gently like the contouring sand of a sunny beach. Your body rests as though it has found the perfect bed. The flow of your breath is natural as you find the rhythms of the inhale and exhale to be the flow of a gentle breeze.

In this peaceful place of earthen comfort, you notice your body's pressure points where they come in contact with the surface below, and you melt further into your support. Everything you need is provided for you in this bed of nourishment.

Your mind wanders into your heart and finds a small packet of seeds. The packet opens effortlessly, and a tiny seed floats into your consciousness. The potential of this small seed calls to you and asks for your direction. You name the seed to represent a deep desire from within your soul—the words of your intention file into the DNA of the cell.

The seed is now ready to be planted.

You bless the seed with hope and invite it to take refuge in your heart. It has been planted within you.

Here, in the soil of your being, you care for the small seed. You keep your heart open to the light. You allow the rain waters and the nutrients from your life to cultivate its burgeoning growth.

Knowing that a precious new life has been planted in the soil of your soul, you take a moment to scan the bed where it has been planted. This seed of potentiality will continue to grow as you love and care for it.

You rise slowly from your place of warmth and comfort and move forward with a pregnant glow of knowing something beautiful is about to sprout and unfurl in your life.

The potential held in the seed cracks through the sheltering cover and thrusts itself into the environment beyond. Then, finally, it is ready to unfurl.

The time has come for integration into the garden of life.

The resistance has been broken, and the yearning for connection takes precedent.

The seedling has emerged, ready for profound growth and expansion.

Chapter 7

THE ROOTS PUSH THROUGH

When packing for the vision fast expedition, I had included an incredibly unique ball of blue yarn with spots of bright colors woven throughout its entirety. Not many people would have bothered to pack a ball of yarn in their backpacking gear, but it was a seed I planted, an intention that I brought with me on my journey. The giant web I ultimately created, strewn between two giant bushes in the woods, was not organized and patterned as we typically think of a web, but it was wide and complicated, with connections running throughout. I found the perfect location to create this web right next to my solo spot. It was life-sized, and I was able to climb into the center of it and reflect on the intricacies, twists, and turns of my life.

As I contemplated the intricacy of the web, I recognized that it represented the systems of communication and connections in life. I envisioned the root systems of the trees in the forest, the neural networks in the brain, and the network of people in my life as webs where messages are relayed from one hub to another. In my web of yarn, these hubs were bright spots of color, and I imagined sparks of energy occurring at these points of connectivity. Further contemplation led me to wonder how the signaling systems of life change and adapt to the messages they are receiving.

For the ball of yarn to have its potential unleashed and go from a seed of inspiration to an art installation in the woods, I had to act on it and interact with it. To further understand the metaphorical seeds of potentiality, I considered the life cycle of nature once again. What signal prompts the seeds of the plant to push through the outer shell and sprout? The environment of its planting generates this growth. The nourishment of the soil, the water it receives, and the warmth of the sunlight hitting the top layer of the soil all call to the plant cell's DNA to adapt, respond, and bring forth new life.

Connections

You can create, cultivate, and celebrate this same life cycle of growth with the potential held within the cells of your human system. If you imagine the neural network in your brain is like yarn strewn from one branch to another and then back again, you are starting to see the web of neurons within your brain. Neurons are fascinating cells. They are found throughout the entire body. They have different structures, and they are the essential communicators regarding our internal and external environment. When you look at their structure, they are like the seeds we're talking about throughout this book. Their dendritic roots push through the organic layers of our tissues and organs. They send messages of communication through electrical and chemical signals, setting off a cascade of essential functions. This network of communication is changing and shifting regularly.

Decades of research have unveiled that our brain is not static and unmalleable—it can change and shift according to the input it receives. This remapping of the connections within the brain is referred to as neuroplasticity. I first came across this research during my master's program, which was based in transpersonal psychology. We studied mindfulness and the impact these practices can have on the patterns of signals produced in our nervous system. The fascinating discovery is that our thoughts influence the pathways and networks in our brain. Sharon Begley, the well-known science writer I referenced earlier, pored over years of research. The journey neuroscience has taken in its own story of plasticity and change from the model of a brain set in its ways to one that can learn and adapt is inspiring. What the research shows is: "The brain remakes itself throughout life in response to outside stimuli—to its environment and to experience" (Begley 2008, 129).

The beauty of neuroplasticity is that thoughts and patterns, even ingrained habits, can change. What neuroplasticity teaches us is that the neural networks that drive our daily functions can change and adapt. From a child's early growth and development to an individual rehabilitating from a stroke, the plasticity of the brain and the nervous system is a phenomenon worth exploring. To understand these networking powerhouses, we can take a closer look at the two main communication tools of the neuron: the axon and the dendrite. The axon carries the electrical signals or impulses and then releases a chemical cloud of neurotransmitters. The potential of our body to carry out any function it needs depends on the messages from these tiny cells. For example, a message relaying that my coffee is brewing comes along the axon and signals an olfactory cell. Then the olfactory signal lets my brain know I can go forage for a cup and pour a hot mug of morning brew. It then recruits other neurons by relaying that message through their dendrites onto their neighbors so my muscles, my heart, my lungs can do everything in their power to move me toward getting the cup of coffee. This example shows how profound our nervous system is and the interplay between our internal and external environments.

When we see that our habits—like grabbing a morning cup of coffee—are a cascade of signals that have the potential to change, their power to hold us fades. We can stand back and witness the patterns produced by signals and the responses that result. This is our inner scientist coming alive and recognizing the alchemy of our thinking, emotions, and actions. They are all connected in the complexity of our humanity—and they have the capacity to change. Yet, how do acceptance and neuroplasticity unite to promote the emergence of the sprouting thought, idea, or dream wanting to manifest in our life? By seeing and allowing the magnificence of our humanity to unfold. Neuroplasticity occurs organically as our perspective and mindset shift. Resilience and adaptability arise from recognizing what we have the power to change and what is beyond our influence.

Knowing that our neurons communicate about external and internal influences, we see that our perceptions regulate the brain. We create images of ourselves and those we interact with in the world around us. These pictures of who we are and how others may respond influence our connectivity. Just as the neurons are relaying messages in our nervous system, we are relaying messages in our ecosystem. The energy we emit and receive affects our overall sense of well-being and our relationships with people. Just as the neuron communicates with an action potential that sparks and releases a neurochemical message, our affect toward others impacts our interpersonal interchanges. Seeing these internal and external connections helps us understand that we are creating, cultivating, and celebrating our lives on a moment-to-moment basis simply by how we show up and live life.

How we cultivate our lives influences how our creative potential manifests. The metaphor of the garden, the plants, and the seeds is powerful because our mind's eye can see the sprout push through the tough outer layer of a seed and manifest as new growth. In this same way, our innate creative force pushes our ideas, hopes, and dreams into the physical realm of existence. We cultivate the emergence of this new growth by connecting to the activities, people, and places that will help it grow. This nourishment in the soil of our lives is what sustains the growth of the seedling.

What are you creating and cultivating in your life? What wants to push through, take root, and grow? Allow yourself to move freely into the flowing current where the focus of creative energy can arise from an openness to uncertainty and give way to a sense of timelessness. When the vision comes to you, dance with it and let it come alive—this is your seed of potentiality. Remove the obstacles by letting go and see the clearing, the open space in your life where you can plant this seed. Turn the soil of your soul, amend it with nourishment, and plant your seed. Now that you have traveled these steps in the life cycle of personal growth, the roots push through, and you grow your potential.

Our connectivity contributes to the growth of our seeds of potentiality. The more we concentrate our awareness on what we want to manifest, the more our brain rallies around this cause and recruits the circuitry in its favor. This reorganization is made feasible by the neuroplasticity of our synaptic connections and creates a harmonization of the neural network. This understanding takes us back to the axiom we explored in the dance of synchronicity: neurons that fire together, wire together. The cultivation of our ideas, hopes, and dreams that we would like to see take root in our lives starts with the remapping of the root system in our brains. What connections are you feeding?

The joyous synchronicity of connections that build upon this collaboration of like-minded neuronal sparks flying through the tissues of our body helps build our resilience. I like to think of resilience as our emotional immune system. While the axons "talk" and the dendrites "listen," our essential communication system creates a framework for dealing with the challenges we face. The beauty of this system is that it is working and flowing all the time. There is no need to put forth mental effort. We do not need to squeeze or force our thoughts in a particular direction. Instead, we can travel back to the peace and refuge found at the bank of the babbling brook and allow the peace and flow of life to connect us to the rivers and streams that will carry us to our desired destination.

Cultivate your vision, nurture yourself, and allow the fabric of life to provide the network you need to generate the synchronous firing of sparks. These sparks are the neurochemistry of being in the flow of life. Continuously connect to the creative outlets that pull you into this flow. Where does creative energy come from in your life? When you connect with that current, allow it to contribute to the nourishment of your growth.

If you are stuck in a thicket of mental entanglement, the concept of neuronal pruning allows connections that are not reinforced to fade. Letting go of connections that do not work is a form of mental composting. Consider again what you are feeding your garden. Does it add to the growth? Or does it put a strain on the new buds trying to unfurl and forge their way in life? Being mindful of what news you read, the social media you engage in, and the people you're in contact with is important for clearing the space needed for growth. Some of these messages may be pulling apart the fabric of your essential being. By selecting the input that edifies and nourishes your ideas, hopes, and dreams, you can grow your internal garden in a way that blossoms into the foliage that brings you joy and peace. Here, in this state of peace, you emerge as a fully blooming human ready to share your potential with those in your family, circle of friends, and community.

The ecosystem of people in your life is the garden where you can grow. Your roots continue to connect and expand, and the plant—the idea, hope, or dream—that has sprouted can feed on the metaphorical sunlight and air of the environment. The connections to sustaining nourishment will continue to support the natural evolution of personal growth. This support is all a part of the continuum of the life cycle.

Emergence

We began this journey with the grandmother tree and explored the potential held in seeds. The beauty of evolving from something so small and seemingly inert into the magnificent display of strength and might as a tree is a time-honored metaphor for growth in our human lives. Spending time in the natural world and witnessing the perpetual life cycle of nature helps us understand how our evolution depends on our interaction with the ecosystem of our environment.

One of the draws to the Ventana Wilderness where I experienced my pilgrimage in the forest is the redwoods. This region is the southernmost tip of their growth along the Oregon and California coasts. To be in their presence is awe-inspiring. The story of their expansion and growth began at the forest floor. For the conifers of this region, they began as a small cone carrying the seeds of their genesis. These seeds, once given the right conditions, took root and grew into a powerful presence. The significance of their life cycle teaches us about our seeds of potentiality and how the roots can push through struggles and strife into a display of inspiring emergence.

The layer between atmosphere and forest life is called the emergent layer because it represents an interaction between the forest and the environment beyond. In both my own life and in the lives of those I've coached, mentored, and witnessed, there is an extremely poignant interface between ourselves and the outside world. Why is this so significant? Because our inherent nature is to be communal. Feeling safe in our communities is crucial for finding peace in our personal lives and the world in which we live. Our environment is where we emerge and the sustenance of where the roots push through.

This balance between internal and external realms connects with the garden metaphor perfectly. When we consider the conditions—the seed needs to push through the outer covering and unlock the potential held within—we can see intrinsic and extrinsic factors at play. The corn seeds I planted with my son this spring illustrate this process. Corn is the type of seed that allows us to universally conceptualize its shape and color, which may help visualize its presence in two different states in the garden. In the bed where we planted these seeds over a month ago, beautiful green shoots are now emerging into the garden.

In contrast, there are still a handful of corn seeds in a jar in my son's playhouse, which has become his outdoor science lab. These seeds are still dormant and hold their potential within. The seeds require specific environmental factors to break through and move from their sleep into a brilliant display of plant life. Our potential as humans can also awaken and breakthrough into a vibrant and flourishing life. Consider your garden—connect to the impact your choice of nourishment has on your health and your ability to emerge.

This capacity to push through, emerge, and change into something new is seen throughout nature. Therefore, the natural world can be a profound teacher because it reveals the innate ability for change. From snowflakes in winter storms to butterflies fluttering free from their cocoons in the spring, we witness the power of transformation and creation. It's the unfolding of pure potential. You have this potential waiting to blossom. Take a moment to connect with what is coming alive in your life.

This aliveness can be as simple as connecting with the power of your breath or the capacity to slow down and observe the unfolding of natural processes. Imagine that the web of neurons in your body is like the root system of a plant. As the neurons take in information and relay messages to the brain, the plant's roots take in information—in the form of nutrition from the soil—to help the plant grow. Your neurons are taking in data and helping support the functions of your body. These are the inherent actions of the physical realm. Once again, we see that our physical health supports our emotional and spiritual health.

The breath you are taking now brings oxygen to your brain and your body. When you bring awareness to that breath, you slow down and connect with the physical act of breathing. In the awareness of your breath, your neurons recognize that you are calm, and they naturally shift to support your relaxed physical state and, therefore, support a quiet mind. When your body and mind are relaxed, your capacity to see and connect with community expands. This connection is the interface between you and the world around you. This expansion is where your spirit and essence emerge and interact with the ecosystem of your life.

A sprout emerges from the small seed that was planted. As it is nourished, the plant grows deeper and taller. The sprout feels the strength of the energy it's receiving from the nourishment it receives above and below. Imagine the nutrients coming to the roots, the sunlight creating photosynthesis, and water bringing vibrance to the plant. These processes fortify the sprout and enable it to reach out into the environment that surrounds it. When we tap into the processes that nourish and fortify our lives, we can emerge with our ideas, artistry, and concepts. Fear may arise and hold us back. When resistance arises, think back to the processes we have discussed throughout the book and consider how to unfurl and allow your potential to break through the shell and take root, despite the resistance. Observe the interface between your internal and external realms. How do you interact with your ecosystem? Taking time to reflect and understand what is happening both internally and externally in your life will help your potential to break through. The witnessing of your life brings insight.

How do we bear witness to our own lives? We slow down, give ourselves space, and observe the inherent ability to adapt, change, and move with the currents of life. When we resist life and the natural processes unfolding, we become stuck. When we are stuck, it becomes difficult to create new ways of being in the world. When we let go, the creative energy that we find in the flowing current arises, and we begin to move forward again. Emergence requires movement, and this momentum comes from allowing life to live through us.

Acceptance

Developing this book was a process of emergence in my life. It took the entirety of my life experiences to construct the framework of insights and ideas shared in the book. The vision fast, pharmacy school, exploring psychology and mindfulness, gardening, painting, friendships, marriage, birthing a child—they all played a role in the fabric of life woven together in this story. Yet, a thread runs through all these experiences that provided me with the opportunity for growth. What carried me through the fear and uncertainty was acceptance.

How do we learn the art of acceptance? We can once again turn to metaphors of nature. The monarch caterpillar spins the chrysalis and emerges as a beautiful butterfly. The tadpole simply transforms with time and becomes a frog. The snowflake falls freely through the air, allowing the crystal structure to form organically from the physical reactions occurring instantaneously in flight. All these processes occurred naturally. They were not forced. The butterfly, the frog, and the snowflake accepted their emergence into a new form. Our metamorphosis may not be as apparent to our eyes as these examples. Still, to allow our seeds of potentiality to emerge into their fullness, we must allow the innate beauty of our inherent creativity to burst forth and illuminate our lives. Acceptance is a discipline, an awareness, that allows for the evolution of our potential to come into full expression.

The awareness developed through acceptance slows the ever-spinning reality of life just enough to gain clarity and opens the door to the cultivation of creativity. Do we move forward, do we stay stuck, or do we step back? If we choose to dance with the synchronicity of life, we find our alignment and connect with our authenticity. When we make this connection, the action potential of life propels us forward, and we are again flowing with the current and remembering the call of the babbling brook. This continuum is the life cycle of personal growth. By constantly letting go and dissolving resistance, our potential emerges, and our hearts soar.

Connecting with our authenticity and experiencing the life cycle of personal growth helps us emerge from the mental fog that settles in when we are overwhelmed with life. When the fog bank clears and we reconnect with our path, the cultivation of our growth continues. It can be a slow process or a sudden awakening. These times of darkness are a normal part of our humanity. By simply knowing that we do not need to lose ourselves in the darkness, we see the flicker of light that connects us to the path forward. The illumination may be dim, yet our impressive neural network knows how to forge new connections, and the glow grows brighter. Attending to this spark of light, putting our focus and attention there, helps it grow brighter. Following this fine thread of light creates the tether to the clearing where we can arrive again at our true essence and flourish without denying the pain that we may have experienced on our life journey.

The interplay between the potential held within and the environment that surrounds the emerging sprout is vital. What do you experience when you emerge from a place of introspection and contemplation? What do you bear or bring forth from the garden within? What potential is wanting to break through you? Do you feel like the sprout awakening to a new environment? For something to emerge from within, there is a beginning—the genesis of growth. This emerging life form is the seed of potentiality. The turning of the soil brought the necessary nourishment, and as we open to the light and quench our thirst in the sunrise of the garden, our cultivation will continue. The nourishment we added—the love, the food, the self-care—provides the conditions needed for growth. The biology of any living thing is rooted in the chemical reactions happening within its cells. The ecosystem of our life influences these reactions.

The creative force held within the seed is brought to life by the cultivation of its emergence. Your emergence is your expression of this creativity in your life, and the cultivation of this spark, this seedling, sustains your growth. The roots do not continue to exist without the upward expression of the flower or tree. Your internal terrain is not the only part of you—you have a physical body in a material world. The outward expression of the plant is seen in the leaves, the fruit, or the flowers it bears. Your interface with friends, family, and community is like the branches, leaves, and flowers of your life. You are integrated with your environment. Seeing the importance of both your internal connections and your relationship with the world demonstrates your inherent interconnectedness.

Growth

The growth I experienced from my rite of passage in the wilderness did not simply come from being out in nature and spending time by myself. It was also cultivated by the people who journeyed with me. This aspect of cultivation is an important benefit to traveling life with others. Our social support systems influence our emotional health and well-being. It's not only the roots and the outward expansion; it's also the interaction with the environment around us that impacts our overall state of peace. This interaction with our environment is the ecosystem of our personal growth.

The ecosystem of our lives includes both the internal and external environments. We have explored our internal terrain and the intricacies that help the seeds of potentiality form and come to life. When the roots push through the internal world and interface with the external world, what will our sprouting seed of potential encounter? What influences our growth? We explored nourishment in the turning of the soil, and we will look at how we can open to the light and thrive in the sunshine in the garden. At this juncture, I want us to contemplate the overall ecosystem. To do this, we will consider what constitutes an enriching environment, the direction of our growth, and our resilience. First, let us define the ecosystem.

An ecosystem is defined as the interaction between various organisms and their physical environment. When we apply this term to our personal lives and how we grow, we picture the other "organisms" we encounter in our environment. One of the prominent organisms in the physical realm of our lives is the people who surround us. From our family to our friends and coworkers, the social realm of the environment can significantly impact our growth. There is only a small degree of choice in who populates our garden of life. This impact of the environment is true in the various natural ecosystems of the planet as well. The cohabitants have a strong tendency to influence our emotional and spiritual lives. Hopefully, we can find solid and supportive friends and mentors.

In my personal journey, these role models taught me that it's okay to make mistakes and learn from them. I was given the container and framework needed to explore and express myself as I grew and gained confidence in who I am. I lived in a community of people who supported my growth and taught me to communicate with love and authenticity. The interactions with family, friends, and teachers shaped my development.

Who are the people in your life who have influenced your growth? Have they been individuals in your native garden, or have you transplanted yourself in a new environment to find encouragement and community? Learning to both seek out edifying relationships and respond to others with love is key to establishing an enriching social environment. These behaviors are internal aspects of how we adapt and interface with the ecosystem.

This adaptation is dependent upon our resilience. Our inner terrain gives rise to how we exchange energy with the people, places, and things in the world around us. However, the circumstances of any given situation may be out of our control; how we react influences the ecosystem of our life. Therefore, the health of our internal environment is vital to the health of our interplay with the external environment. When we approach life with a deep level of acceptance, the internal rhythm and flow influence our movement with the external realm.

Your resonance with your ecosystem creates spherical growth. Not only are you reaching deep into the soil below and up to the light above, but you are also interfacing with the environment of your garden. Growth is multidimensional. The solutions for a healthy garden depend on growth in the physical, emotional, social, and spiritual planes of life. Self-awareness helps you to be the observer and the gardener. You can recognize what generates wellness in these various dimensions and adjust and expand your conscious approach to life. By stepping back and evaluating your growth process, you see that you are not trying to take down the complex web of life but are looking to understand your relationship to its magnificence.

Celebrating our challenges is just as important as celebrating our successes. When we take the time to see the intricacies of life and the people in our web of life, we may catch the glimmer of hope and renewal that rests on simply our perspective. The stories of people who have overcome are inspiring and remind us that we can rise robustly from the lessons we learn along the way. All the influential women in my life have overcome struggles and hardship. From difficult childhoods to health issues, they have grown and persisted in their evolution. They took their calling and passion and transformed their lives. Their seeds of potentiality did not lie dormant. Instead, they rose through the fires of their lives and blossomed in full expression of their beauty.

Cultivating all directions of our growth develops an integrated state of well-being. In this homeostasis with our environment, we reach a place of contentment. How do we cultivate our growth? By continuing to move through the life cycle of personal growth. We look to the continuum of planting anew, pruning and composting, and celebrating what grows. As our garden emerges, the roots connect with the nutrients in the soil, and our new growth comes to life. In the life cycle of personal growth, this is a time in our cultivation to move beyond challenges and flourish! As we bloom into our fullness, we become ready to celebrate the sunrise in the garden. The roots that pushed through have made connections in the soil below, and the sprout of potential expands in all directions.

The Roots Push Through Meditation

You are standing on soft soil, connected with the earth that supports you.
The cool touch of the earth on your bare feet awakens an awareness within.
Slowly, you see tendrils growing from the soles of your feet into the earthen floor that twist and curve through the barriers below.
These roots push through the obstacles and forge paths of stability and support.
Once these connections are established, you envision the nurturance of the soil feeding up through the roots into your being. You feel fortified and stand tall. The lengthening of your spine invites a deep breath that rises and falls in your chest.
You are expanding in all directions, creating a spherical connection with the world around you. You glow. And then you begin to grow.
Your arms stretch out and reach beyond their imaginable length, and your heart opens. Here, in this space of expansive growth, you connect with the energetic flow of your potential.
The potential surges through your being, and its manifestation creatively rises through your root bed.
Here in your pulsating beauty, you feel complete, content. You linger a moment longer to feel the fullness of your present state.
Slowly, you scoop the energy that surrounds you, and you gently bring it to your heart center. Hands resting on your heart, you breathe deeply.
You are home, embodied in your wholeness.

The gate creaks open, and there is the melody of a bluebird that harmonizes with the song of the hinges. A path leads down a slope to a brilliant display of fruits, trees, vegetables, and vines. The light filters through the oaks and illuminates the dawn.

It is a place of magic and mystery, where the hum of bees reverberates across the landscape and holds the promise of the sweet taste of honey.

This is a place of opening, where thirst can be quenched, and the heart stands in awe of creation.

Chapter 8

SUNRISE IN THE GARDEN

By the third day of my vision fast, I was settled in and felt comfortable with my surroundings. The fresh air, the birds, the trees (the grandmother tree in particular), and the rocks had become my friends. I could hear the whispering of the wind and observe the swaying of the branches as I considered the life of these forest giants who had become my friends. I felt at peace and was in awe of what I had discovered and encountered, not only in the natural terrain but in the depths of my internal terrain. As I looked out at the view from my solo spot and drew in the magnificence, I recognized the need to carry this sense of awe back into daily life.

Like a lizard on a hot rock, I found a place of warmth along the outer perimeter of my solo spot. The rock was enormous and stately. It was like a lookout tower that stood solidly atop the hillside. It was here on this pinnacle that I let the afternoon sunlight warm my body and soul. I was thankful to have found this spot where I could open my heart and melt my worries. The process of digging deep and connecting within needed the balance of being free and relaxing into the beauty I was witnessing. My heart was opening and my thrist for a deep internal connection was being quenched. Here in the warmth of the sunshine I felt the awe of embracing the gift of this time with myself.

Opening to the Light

Balancing the time for introspection with the time it takes to care for oneself is vital for our growth. When we contemplate the internal landscape of peaks and valleys, sometimes we come across caves where we have hidden parts of our lives. What do you do with these aspects of life you would rather forget? The process of bringing hidden thoughts, memories, or feelings into the light can be exhausting, and we may prefer to ignore them. So the challenge is to figure out how to integrate these cave-dwelling creatures of our souls into the bliss of new growth. Do we cast them out? If so, where do they go? The solution is in how we cultivate our garden of life.

When we cultivate a physical garden, we consider the amount of sunlight and water a particular plant needs and then care for it accordingly. We also prune back the withering branches and fading foliage. The same cultivation is needed for our internal garden. In the life cycle of personal growth, the process of letting go continues, and it may be time to set the cave creatures free. Other hindrances in our internal gardens may be like bugs or pests we're unable to eradicate, so we learn how to deter them from eating the tender leaves of lettuce and the fresh strawberries. In the garden of our lives, we can find ways to shift our focus and reinforce positive pathways through neuroplasticity. The internal bugs are reprogrammed, and their nuisance fades as we focus on the gratitude for what is growing in the garden of our soul. Nature is a truly beautiful metaphor for our internal landscape that we can grasp and envision.

You may be wondering what to do with the persistent creepy-crawly thoughts and feelings that run around inside. The buggy internal aggravations will be less of a burden if we expose them to the light. Turn the rock over and allow the sunlight to bring a fresh perspective. The creatures of the dark will scatter, our awareness will shift, and the process of opening to the light will stimulate a dynamic internal ecosystem. By being resilient and responsive to the illumination, we change. Our innate creativity nourishes our ability to cultivate this new vision by using the tools of self-care that we discovered along our journey. We become master gardeners of the patch of land that our consciousness has been given to cultivate.

Connecting with our gratitude is a way of celebrating this garden of life.

As we explored previously, keeping a gratitude journal can be a tool to aid in this shift of perspective. It becomes your gardening notebook where you can record what is working in the cultivation of your garden. A written record—or an illustrated record—may be useful for remembering what you've been thankful for and encouraging you as you tend to your garden of life. What pests did you encounter? How did you attract the pollinators that helped your garden thrive? What solutions did you find for the changes of the seasons? In your journal, note the successes and failures—both are celebrations in the process of growth. These notes become your rings of remembrance. By looking back on your progress and reflecting on your process, your awareness expands.

When reviewing the notes of my gratitude journal, I realized that the people in my life are the metaphorical sources of sunlight in my internal garden. The people we interact with and the communities we live in are wonderful sources of light. Are we letting that light into the garden of our souls? We are a social species that thrives on interactions with others. Consider the people in your life who are the beacons of light and hope. How do you tend to these relationships? Are you reaching out and staying connected? One of my friends and I went one step beyond our gratitude journals and began sending each other daily gratitude texts. It was a fun way to stay connected and share what we were thankful for. This practice was helpful while we were both going through the growth process of being moms with young, energetic boys. Our friendship evolved, and we were reminded that we could find sunshine even in the storms of life.

Another source of light that supports and nurtures our growth is our spiritual life. Finding communities of individuals looking to reflect upon the practices that stimulate our growth and awareness can bolster our ability to open to the light. Many paths allow us to explore and embrace the mysteries of the universal fabric of life. What understanding resonates with you? Is it life-affirming and leading you to a greater connection to the currents and energies that carry and sustain you? What encourages you when life feels stormy and gray?

Some days we do not see the sunrise. The weather blocks its rays. On these days, it takes a shift to see the source of light is available within. We may tend to chase the sun rather than accept the current conditions, and this is when tension rises. This conflict within describes our mental chase for the positive. Why are there days when I have a foggy brain? Why can't my mental landscape feature blue skies every day? We strive, and we push to clear out the fog, only to find it rolling back in. What if we accepted the lack of clarity and delighted in the game of the fog and the sun playing tag? When the sun is there, let the light in. When you can't see it, recognize it's present but out of view for the moment. The more we see that the fog and the sunshine are constants in our lives, our inner light grows. We glow with awareness, and the glow is there even in the fog. These are the rhythms and the melodies in our lives that help us accept the natural patterns.

When I was living in the Monterey Bay area, which is known for its dense, heavy fog, I found myself in this game of sunshine tag. There are days when the fog and the sun play with each other, and the sun shifts as the fog rolls in and out over the coastline. On my days off, I would spend my time chasing the sun, trying to find the perfect place to hike, journal, or enjoy a picnic outside. I was focused on what I could attain from the outside. On the days it was sunny everywhere, I was not focused on this chase because the sunshine was ubiquitous. When I was in the fog, I was drawn to the patches of blue sky. This frenzied search for the physical rays of light reminded me of my internal quest for continuous joy and happiness from something outside myself. What I learned was that contentment came from cultivating a vibrant glow in my soul.

Accepting the natural patterns of life is the ability to accept duality: to see the black and the white and embrace the shades of gray in between. Too often, we try to make everything perfect and feel defeated when we can't. Instead of striving for perfection, stand in the present moment and allow the hidden sources of light to become apparent. The rays of light are glowing from within. Recognizing this internal radiation warms our hearts and connects us to our human experience. When we open the shutters and doors of our lives and welcome the warmth of the sun into the nooks and crevices of the internal landscape, we satisfy an internal need to feel connected.

Quenching Thirst

Thirst helps keep us hydrated and is a vital aspect of our survival. Maintaining a clean water supply was a part of my daily routine during the vision fast. I treated the water from the babbling brook with iodine tablets, which turned the clear, cool liquid a murky brown color and gave it an astringent taste. Since I was only drinking water during the fast, I recognized the importance this water held for my health, and my reverence increased for the sole substance I had at the time. But I wondered, where did the water in my happy little brook come from? What would happen if I didn't have this water?

Recognizing the resources that revitalize and sustain us is key to our health. Our health is vital to our growth. We have learned that the process of amending the soil of our lives influences our physical, emotional, and spiritual well-being. When we consider the food, feelings, thoughts, and beliefs we consume, our awareness of what revitalizes us and drains us becomes more apparent. What brings vitality to the attributes of our soil? Hydration. We need a universal solvent to keep the soil of our soul from drying out.

When we consider the importance and mysteries of water, we are also learning about one of the key molecules in our lives. Why? Because we are physically made of around 60 percent water. If we dig deeper, we can see the life-sustaining role water plays in the functionality of our internal systems. Hydration is necessary for life. Returning to our nature metaphors, the simple biology of a plant teaches a valuable lesson about the vitality water provides in the picture of health. Plant cells contain a large vacuole to hold water. When a plant is deprived of water, that vacuole shrinks. It shrinks in all the cells of the plant, and the plant wilts. When we do not attend to the basic needs of life, we wilt. Our wilting may be not only physical but also emotional and spiritual. How do we keep from wilting? We stay hydrated physically, emotionally, and spiritually.

How will you fill your cup? What resources are present in your life that can replenish you? When we recognize our physical, emotional, or spiritual thirst, we can quench it; how we choose to satiate our thirst influences our well-being. For example, are you choosing life-affirming hydration? Hydration is meant to decrease the toxic substances in our bodies. Considering how you are quenching your thirst will help you recognize if you are adding to the internal toxicities that build up from life or if you are helping to move them through and process them.

First, let's quench our physical thirst. Did you know that following a simple routine of two glasses of water in the morning activates your organs, one glass before each meal aids digestion, one before your bath or shower lowers blood pressure, and one before bed helps your heart? This regimen is seven of your recommended eight daily glasses! Add one more when you get off work or before you pick up the kids from school, and you have a fantastic hydration schedule.

You can create similar patterns in your process of emotional hydration. What do you crave in your life? What drives your emotional thirst? The body has innate systems that drive our desires, but emotions can influence our tendency to seek immediate gratification. It's amazing how challenging attending to our basic needs can be! We try to accomplish so much on little sleep, stressed relationships, and poor food sources. Imagine if we were running on full nights of sleep, harmonious interactions, and revitalizing food. We could change the world—and we still can. By considering our choices and whether we are quenching our basic need for water or satisfying a need for immediate gratification, our lives can shift.

The refreshment that water provides the physical body also aids the natural processes needed to flourish spiritually. When you feed your soul with mindful moments and gratitude, your spiritual cup fills with a vitality that brings renewal and sustainment. You are tending to the garden of your life by watering the seeds of your soul through any of the restorative practices that we have explored throughout the book. From connecting with others to journaling your gratitude, you can find ways that fill the vacuoles of your heart and spirit. When these places of figurative hydration are swelling with life-sustaining substances, your life feels vibrant, and your energy pulses with the vibration of a well-watered being.

Since we recognize its crucial importance, how do we learn to be good stewards of the water? These are critical questions we may not be taking the time to consider. For those of us fortunate to have a clean water supply, we may not recognize the perils of unclean water until we experience a natural disaster, have water supply maintenance issues in our neighborhood, or go backpacking in the wilderness and need to clean the water supply ourselves. Being aware that water is a precious resource in our world opens us to understanding our connection to the natural world and the universal need for this invaluable asset.

Just as we are exploring our life cycle of personal growth, water also has its life cycle. Have you ever considered that all water is currently present in the water cycle? It simply changes forms between a liquid, solid, or gas and moves through our atmosphere, snow-capped mountains, and oceans. In the same way, all the resources for your life cycle are entirely present. Some of them may simply be in an unrecognizable form. The importance of understanding life cycles is to point out that the entirety of a global resource is present in the water cycle, and the entirety of the resources you need are present in your personal life cycle. Everything you need for life is already in existence.

Awe

I now realize the story of my time in the wilderness provides a portal into the garden of my life. There are many portals one can use for introspection. When we stop and see the vistas from the couch in our home, we can also be in awe. It's not only the natural world on the outside that we are taking in with a full and nourishing breath but also the internal landscape that can offer as much beauty and brilliance as the outside.

Your seeds of potentiality have grown and blossomed, filling the internal terrain with a lush landscape. The garden will need to be maintained with the soil, water, and sunlight we have explored. If we have come to love and adore that internal garden, it will not feel like a tedious task or something to put on the to-do list. The tending of the garden will become an innate practice of self-care. The joy of drinking water, eating healthful food, and exposing ourselves to the light will sustain us. And there, in the warm glow, we can feel a sense of awe.

I spent a lot of time—years, actually—trying to find this feeling of contentment. I read books, attended seminars, bought apps for my phone, joined various groups, and climbed to the tops of mountains. There is nothing wrong with any of these tools or resources. But what finally made a difference was when I learned to shift my perspective. Rather than looking for something on the outside to nourish, calm, or help me achieve my goals, I turned within. I found the seeds of potentiality that grew into a more vibrant, full, and rewarding life than I would have realized if I had kept focusing outward.

What are the moments in your life when you have been in awe? For my husband and me, the birth of our son, Declan, was an awe-inspiring moment. The miracle of life springing forth and entering the world is a moment imprinted on me forever. Our physical genesis is a miracle and not something to take for granted. We also experience times of emotional and spiritual birth when we enter a new understanding or perspective of how we conceptualize and move with the events of life.

When we connect with the mystery and magic woven into the fabric of our lives, the noise of the busy world can drop away and fade into the distance. The chatter can lighten and transform into the sweet sounds of children playing or the rustling of leaves. Let the flowing current carry you and the sounds of life into the unknown. Do you feel the peace of surrendering and flowing with the synchronicities of life? As you allow your senses to experience the unfolding of life, take a moment to acknowledge the awe of your presence in the world—you are significant.

Every life on earth holds significance. When we begin to value life with this level of respect and honor, our perspectives can shift. Your neighbor, your family, your friend, and your perceived adversary are all sacred. Standing in awe is a portal to seeing the divine light that weaves through our existence. It is the light that illuminates as energy currents run throughout our nervous system. It is the unfolding of the cascades of signals and messages that pulse throughout our bodies. When we truly stop and recognize the masterpiece of our existence, how can we not stand in awe?

I hope that you will find ways to connect with the inspiration that contemplating humanity invokes. Whether it's learning more about the physicality of how your body works, the emotional complexities of social justice, or the spiritual realms of a particular practice—there is a fascinating continuum that constitutes the structure and the fabric of our daily experience. What makes you who you are? How does knowing the inner depths of your personhood help you connect with others? These are important questions to consider. This questioning relates to your spherical growth—you are expanding in awareness regarding your body, mind, and spirit. This expansion is the blooming of your seeds of potentiality.

The unfurling of our radiance can make a universally positive impact on humanity. I have provided some ideas in the resources section of this book—from physical seeds to tending to the soil of your soul and others—there are ways to give back to the life cycle that sustains you. I want you to connect with what invokes awe in your soul.

For example, my friends Cristin and Peter are in awe of the abundance found in the natural world. They have established a homestead that produces beans, honey, corn, fruit, eggs, and so much more. The rhythms of their lives and their backyard farm are orchestrated by the seasons. Inspiration and beauty are generated from their gardening, foraging, and self-sustaining way of living. Sunrise in their garden is a magical event.

Imagine the sparkle of the sun shining through the dew on the leaf of a corn stalk. This corn stalk is from a seed that has been passed on for generations. It's growing under the canopy of oak trees that have been standing on the land for over a century. The plants in their garden are pollinated by the bees that are cared for and contained in the hives that Cristin and Peter keep on their land. Cherry blossoms adorn the fruit grove in the spring, and you can hear the clucking of the hens as they peck their way through the dry leaves strewn across the damp earth.

Where do you find your awe and magical inspirations? Do you have a small garden to tend to where you can watch plant life blossom and grow? Or maybe there is a particular activity that brings you into your state of flow and creativity? Connect with what brings you alive. From this state of alive awareness, your vision will become crystal clear. Consider a rainbow reflected in a dewdrop and recognize the magnificence of life reflected in the simplest form, the sacred wonders of the world.

One of my favorite daily rituals is my morning walk. It sets the tone for the day by filling my lungs with fresh air and invigorating my whole body. One day while out for my morning jaunt, I encountered the sacred wonder of life in a dewdrop right at eye level. It was a beacon, reflecting life and reminding me that perspective is vital, witnessing the wonders that are ever-unfolding around me. How else do these walks invoke awe and inspiration? The best days are when I make it to the top of the hill in our neighborhood. From this lookout, I can see for miles. When I crest the top of my mini-mountain before sunrise, I delight in seeing the sun peek out over the hills in the distance. My heart floods with the warmth I witness, and I stand in awe of the brilliance of a new day.

The sunrise in the garden of our lives fills us with warmth and satisfaction that we are living life to its fullest potential. This manifestation of attending to the needs of our physical, emotional, and spiritual realms of life results from the cultivation of the growth emerging in our internal terrain. The peace that rises is like the morning song of the birds that provides a sweet melody to the tasks of daily life. In this state of contentment, the process of living in tune with our life cycle of personal growth produces an innate surge of joy. This delight in life is not produced by effort or achievement; it arises from the simplicity of being aware and attending to the moment. Bringing your attention to the moment allows you to quench your thirst and open to the sunlight. This cultivation of your body, mind, and spirit is celebrated in the awe and glory of recognizing the inborn capacity to create your life every day.

Feel the beams of morning light shining into your precious heart. The sun is rising in us each time we awaken to a new dawn. Stand in awe of the light that shines from within. Connect to this internal source of energy that can transform your life. From here, explore what it feels like when the cup runs over, the garden is vibrant with life, and inspiration sets the daily rhythm. It's the joy of abundance.

Sunrise in the Garden Meditation

Your feet feel the soft earth as you slowly open the wooden gate and enter a magical garden. Your breath rises and falls as you take in the awe of the scene before you.

The soft light filters through the trees and rests gently upon an inviting bench. You slowly make your way to the bench and relax into its structure.

Connected with your breath, you scan your internal landscape and notice where you feel most open. It may be your throat, ears, feet, heart, or somewhere unexpected. Wherever you sense that opening, take a moment to push it open wider and look out to see the light.

It is sunrise, and the golden hues of warmth start to pour into that portal. Connect with the sensations of the light coming in. Feel the warmth and comfort of the morning sun.

Allow the glowing essence to move gently through your body. Feel it swirl and glide across your inner landscape. As it expands… thank the light for arriving.

Let it flow where it needs to go. Let the process be natural. Maybe it will open a few more doors and windows. If it encounters a closed door, allow the resistance to pass and just be.

Deeply feel the warmth of the light.

Follow the warm glow throughout your body.

Once the light has moved across the body, sense the arrival of a new moment in time, like a new day dawning.

The light is present, and it has expanded. Take a moment to acclimate to the glow.

Embrace your light.

There is a glow that floats free and tickles the heart of those who allow it entry. It has a spark that is ignited by love and fanned by gratitude.
It may appear as a cup running over or a basket overflowing with the crops of life. From the sounds of the birds to the sweet taste of fresh fruit, it enriches the senses.
The rainbow of light it produces comes from the prism of the soul that is angled precisely right for the full spectrum to shine through.

Chapter 9

THE JOY OF ABUNDANCE

Walking back to base camp with a smile and soot on my face, my multicolored web of yarn woven into a bird's nest and cradled in my matted hair, I knew I had accomplished what I had come to the wilderness for—to reconnect with my authentic self. Having found that connection, I knew I could take life a little less seriously, and my presence proved that true. The guides chuckled when they saw me coming up the trail with my nest bobbing on the top of my head and my heart humming an audible tune. Finally, we gathered at our metaphorical rabbit hole, where we descended three days earlier to initiate our solo fasts. The reintegration process began as we found our way back, and the joy of regathering filled our hearts.

That night we gathered before a large rock, and everyone took a turn sharing their stories and experience of their solo time. What I noticed about the group was the levity. As we each discovered or rediscovered aspects of ourselves, the weight of trying to be something else lifted. With the veils of society released to the wind and the connections to our potential abounding, we were smiling and laughing with delight. Of course, we were relieved to have some food in our bellies and the companionship of others, yet the lessons we learned while out on our own lightened the loads we had brought with us to the forest. In our stories, you could hear that each of us had found the freedom to follow our soul's yearning and fall in love again with the one person we all knew we would spend the rest of our lives living with, ourselves.

Love

While on my vision fast, I was part of a marriage ceremony. Not in relationship to anyone on the expedition into the woods; a marriage with myself. There was the altar rock to set the stage and the grandmother tree to witness. The music of the babbling brook provided the melody, and the sunlight illuminated the space unlike any church or cathedral could match. It was glorious and divine. I had written vows, adorned myself with the one white shirt I had in my pack, placed a few flowers in my hair, and proceeded with the most important commitment I would ever make in my life: to love myself.

I am a divine being, whole and complete.
In the here and now, I commit myself to thee.
Through the trials and tribulations of life, I will stand by your side.
I will not abandon you.
I will come home daily and be in your presence.
Connected within, I will carry the joys of life into the world.
Centered and complete.
I am yours.

This set of vows is my commitment to myself. By bringing my presence and nurturing love to the care of my body, mind, and soul, I am tending to my life, a garden. The garden that I have the ultimate responsibility to tend and cultivate. The devotion and attention that I put into choosing the foods I eat, the words I speak, and the activities I participate in have a foundational influence on the quality of my days and nights. By finding my creative flow, igniting the fire in the clearing, turning the soil, and allowing my roots to push through, I arrived at the sunrise in the garden of my life with an outpouring of love.

When our approach to daily life is rooted in love, we can reframe our understanding of our interaction with ourselves and others. The compassionate care and loving attention we give to life—to our garden—are vital nutrients for growth. How do we make love the basis of our life? By learning to love ourselves. This self-love is not an ego-driven love; it's an authentic love that comes from understanding that we can love others with acceptance and sincerity. When we think about the fabric that we are woven from—the cells, the tissues, the chemical and electrical impulses—we know that we are all made of the same elemental matter that constitutes all life.

When we live from a place of integrity, our connection to others overflows with fullness, love, and grace. This connection is the thread that runs throughout the fabric of the stories I have shared and connects us to the ever-unfolding life cycle of our development. It's the commitment to loving ourselves and others as the sacred and whole beings that we are. From allowing the façade of our masks to dissolve to riding the flow of the current, we can return to the peace that resides within when we are connected to the power of love. This place of contentment is not a distant land or an elusive destination. It's a wellspring that lives within each of us. Connecting with this internal fountain of peace and hope brings comfort because it feels like coming home.

With an expansive heart, I returned home and reunited with my friends and family. My fiancé at the time—now my incredible husband—greeted me with cards and flowers. He had entrusted the wilderness (and my guides) with my safety. When we remove ourselves from daily life, our return enriches us with a spark of joy and deep gratitude for the people, places, and things that we missed during our journey. There is an element of comfort in love. That cozy feeling of knowing you belong. When you know yourself and find your tribe, your community, the contentment of connection builds. The love you created in your life continues to be cultivated by these relationships and then celebrated in the joy of abundance.

When I first connected with my personal mantra of "create, cultivate, celebrate," I found there were threads of love in each aspect. What did I want to create more of in my life? Love! How would I cultivate the relationships in my life? Love! How would I celebrate the connections that had manifested through creating and cultivating? Love! It was the only word that showed up as an answer to everything. We have heard love is the answer, and it may even sound like a cliché. What happens, though, when you sit with the word love and feel into the significance it holds? How do you define love? For me, it is a warm glow that weaves through the relationships in life.

Love is part of the harvest. It's the fruit of the personal growth journey we explored throughout the book. It may show up in different ways without you even realizing it. It may pop up as a new friendship, a new romantic relationship, or a new community of inspiring people. Love may manifest as an astounding piece of artwork, a book that has been writing itself in your heart for years, or a song that has been waiting to be sung. If not in relationships or creative endeavors, love can surface in the dinner you cook for your loved ones, the thank-you message you send a coworker, or the smile you share with another.

Integrating love into the fabric of our life clothes us with the protection and strength we need to forge through tough times while also allowing us to fully express who we are. The covering of love protects us; it fortifies us. It helps us to withstand the elements. How we present ourselves in the world is an expression of our connection to the protective presence of love. When we are loving, laughing (levity), and growing (expansion), we are living in the joy of abundance.

Shifting Our Mindset

The stresses of life are real, and the struggles we face are mountainous. When we connect with the light we hold and the seeds of potentiality within, we can shift our perspectives. The circumstances do not change; we do. As the monks and mindfulness experts have taught us, we can train our brains. One way to think of this training or perspective shift is the concept of a growth mindset. Carol Dweck wrote the pivotal book *Mindset: The New Psychology of Success* over a decade ago, and now this is a household term to describe our perceptions. In her book, Carol unpacks success and failure and our human responses to various circumstances. When we have a growth mindset, we believe we can overcome and thrive in the face of struggles.

On the other hand, if we have a fixed mindset, we will more likely give up and find the easiest way out of any given situation. In her book, she states, "Mindsets are just beliefs. They're powerful beliefs, but they are just something in your mind, and you can change your mind" (Dweck 2008, 16). Carol started her studies about the variations in mindset by examining children's responses to puzzles: some thrived and took the challenge head-on while others balked at the exercise. In the opening chapter of her book, she refers to the resilient problem solvers: "These children were my role models. They obviously knew something I didn't and I was determined to figure it out—to understand the kind of mindset that could turn a failure into a gift" (Dweck 2008, 3-4).

This concept that we can learn from our failures and emerge stronger is key to the celebration of our lives. The joy of abundance does not feel as sweet when it comes without struggle and sweat. The dusty trails, the pangs of hunger, and the sleepless nights of my vision fast had a profound impact on my life—it was challenging, and I learned from my struggles. However, when we see the challenges as opportunities, we can push through the outer layers like a seedling emerging from its covering of the seed and display our potential. This recognition that the difficult times are a blessing is a growth mindset. We are celebrating our innate human potential to grow, and we see the gift in failure that the children in Dweck's study were able to inherently see and move beyond.

The other thing that motivated the children to persist through the challenge was the perception that the puzzle was fun. They didn't take the task too seriously; they had a lightness to their mindset, which helped make the difficult task more enjoyable. The root of levity is "lev" in Latin. "Lev" means "lift, be light." I lifted, heaved, and lugged the weight of my heavy backpack over miles during my trek. However, the burden of my pack is not what left a lasting mark on my soul. It's the levity I feel since I walked back into my daily life that carries me forward. To maintain this levity in everyday life, I am constantly refocusing the lens, turning over the rock, and lifting the veil to see that I have a choice. My response can be heavy or light.

Watch and observe your responses to life's challenges. Do they all need to carry the weight you have given them? See the shift and find the flow that comes from responding with levity. This shift in perspective is another lesson I am learning as a mom. My son is overly sensitive. And I am not stating that to give him a pass. But, I am sharing something he inherited from me (both explicitly and implicitly). I can be overly sensitive. He reflects what it looks like when I quickly bristle at the response of others. All the self-help guidance and internal exploration are not as poignant as facing my own struggle. The remedy? Levity—delivered in songs, puppet shows, fables, and more. Who can resist the joy of blowing bubbles, creating chalk art, and chasing rainbows?

Here is a story about my son that illustrates my point. Rainbows danced on the wall as the light shone through the glass in the lamp hanging above our kitchen table. This was my opportunity to shift a meltdown, so I called to him: "Declan, look at the colors and the rainbows. They've come to play with you!" The tears streaming down my son's face stopped, and he slowly came down the hallway to see what his silly momma was trying to show him. We played shadow puppets in the rainbow reflections, and his frustration faded. Whatever precipitated his agony was forgotten. When we pay attention to the rainbows, our hearts can mend and heal as well.

Levity and love are healing balms that soothe wounds like no other medicine I know. Incorporating these salves into your home remedies will bring healing and restore health. Take time to connect with what creates these moments of lighthearted joy in your life. From the music of the babbling brook to the dance of synchronicity, find the melodies and moments that lift and carry you forward. It may be a loving animal that brings you joy or the company of good friends. Use the awareness you have cultivated to surface these gemstones that glitter and glow in your life and honor their importance and soul-reviving medicine.

As you have traveled the pages of this book and the terrain of your heart, what treasures have you found? These are the joys of abundance, and they can be celebrated in the life cycle of your personal growth. The masks have disintegrated, the webs of despair woven into new frameworks, and the fear of uncertainty transformed into a flow with the nature of life. You have cultivated this garden by turning the soil and planting your seeds of potentiality. Now, as the growth expands, you recognize that abundance comes from within.

Expansion

Arms outstretched, I welcome in the joys of the universe. All is coming together. I am living life. Content, compassionate, and creative. Guided by authenticity, awareness, and acceptance. The potential, the releasing, allowing, arriving, digging, growing, opening, quenching all brought me to this moment of absolute bliss. I am not on the mountaintop or on a retreat. I am sitting here writing this book. For you. For me. For humanity. A chill runs down my back because the nirvana of my life is knowing that I am exactly who I am supposed to be. Right now, and in every moment.

Your potential has brought you here. Take a moment to sense any edges. Let them fade. Feel your energy push outward—all of it. Do not hold back. Expand. Shine. Fully express. Connect with the flow, the glow that we have uncovered in this process.

Think of the dandelion seeds swept up and spread by the wind or breath—their vitality reaches beyond the singularity of one wish into a field blooming with hope. There is the potential for a harvest in that field from the cultivation of crops, an orchard, or a vineyard. These crops are the outpouring of your life. Whether you are an agriculturist tending to grapes on a vine, apples in a tree, or carrots in the ground—this is your growth. In the garden metaphor, your abundance flows from the beauty and peace of living and being. This abundance is the celebration of your life.

The abundance of an expanding awareness starts with the seed, with your vision to live authentically. It is then cultivated with the nourishment of presence and perseverance. Time, attention, and love will feed the garden of your soul. Finally, when the garden is overflowing with its bounty, we can share its abundance. It is an outpouring of the lessons you have learned and the joy you feel.

One of the greatest examples of someone living out the joy of abundance is a teacher. Teachers, mentors, and individuals willing to patiently explain the paths and the steps to grow and learn in life are those who are pouring out of the wellspring they have inside. I shared with you several of my teachers throughout this book. Who are the teachers and mentors in your life? Who are you reaching out to for advice and support? Consider who you choose, as it may influence what you decide to plant and cultivate in your garden. There are also unexpected teachers. These may be visitors to the garden who bear a special gift or bring insight to our gardening practices. Our awareness of our response to the wisdom bestowed by others expands our understanding of ourselves. Do we openly accept the advice, or do we close to the external input?

Another group of individuals whose innocence and curiosity teach volumes are children. My most profound teacher is my son. As a mother, I have much to teach and encourage my son to grow, but I never imagined how much I would learn about life and myself from him. Parenting takes more patience than I ever imagined. By learning the skill of slowing down, being present, and watching him grow into an amazing human being, I am learning the deeply rewarding practice of patient presence. We enter this state of presence when our eyes, ears, and hearts are open to receiving the messages carried by the people, circumstances, and shifts in life. The journey through life will continue to evolve and bring new experiences and challenges. When we integrate those learning points into our celebration of life, we continue to grow just as a curious child grows and learns in daily life.

Life cycles are about the continual flow from one stage in our growth to another. When we stand in the joy of abundance, we celebrate the gifts we receive from a well-lived life. Recognizing that the seeds of potentiality have passed through their journey of being creatively conceived, cultivated in the nourishment of our souls, and blossomed with bright vitality, we watch for what new seeds will emerge next in our lives. Will these seeds be the product of the growth we have already embraced and experienced, or will they be new seeds brought forth by continually connecting with our innate creativity? These new seeds will continue the life cycle and continue our human evolvement. Here in the circle of life, we see that our potential expansion has been set into motion. By flowing with the current and encouraged by the melodies of the babbling brook, we continue to turn the soil, plant the seeds of potentiality, and experience a harvest of insight.

The Joy of Abundance Meditation

Your eyes are closed, and you connect with your breath.
Ride the current of your breath and find its flow. Your hands float to your heart center.

Visualize a glowing seed floating between your hands. Ever so slowly, imagine the radiance from the glowing seed gently pushing your hands outward. The seed is growing right before you in midair. The potential unfurls, and the light expands. Joy from witnessing this beauty rises in your heart.

Breathe. Relax your shoulders. Allow the process to unfold.
Feel the expansion.

See this radiance as the seed transforming into a beautiful and vibrant flower.

The process emerges naturally. As your hands reach the outer edges of your body, allow your palms to turn upward gently. Allow your arms to continue to flow outward.

Release the blooming flower.

See it as an offering from your heart.

Send it out.

With your arms still outstretched, pull your energy back in through the top of your head and down into your heart. You are now bathed in this radiance of bliss.

Feel the energy glowing in each of your hands as they scan your body.

Slowly allow your hands to drop toward the ground and offer the energy to the earth.

Once released, carefully and slowly place your hands on your heart. Feel the warmth. Connect with your breath. Allow the energy to flow down your center, a warm glow that drifts down into your hips and then travels through your legs to your feet.

The light you have released planted a garden of abundance, and you are present in that garden—the blades of grass glow and drip with droplets of light.
See the roots, the soil, the earth that supports you.
You are connected to the joy of abundance.

There is a time when the fruits have ripened on the vine, and their fullness calls for gathering. Harvesting fills the basket and represents a fullness that overflows with the gifts received. To fully embrace the taste, the smell, and the delight of the accumulation—take a moment of silence and gratitude to connect the efforts of cultivation, born from creation, into a celebration.

It is a commemoration of all that has preceded this moment in time and a hope for all that will come in the moments ahead.

For it is all a part of the life cycle, the wholeness, the circle of life.

Chapter 10

THE HARVEST OF INSIGHT

When I walked into my living room, I was greeted by the light dancing on the wall. I felt the cool tile beneath my feet supporting me, and I released a huge sigh of relief. The gentle sensation of being home from my vision fast filled my entire being. Traveling with the seeds of potentiality in my life has taken me on journeys I never imagined possible. Now with the insights I gleaned from moving through the stages of creation, cultivation, and celebration, I glow with inner harmony. I feel the reverie and linger with the sensations that arise.

There is a quiet peace that runs throughout my body when my mind filters back to my time in the wilderness. My breath deepens, and I connect with the sensation of solace that holds the ingrained memories of my experience. From the solid support of the earth holding me at the edge of the babbling brook to the deep connection with self in the clearing, I feel alive with authenticity and potentiality. This vibrancy that I brought back from my time in the wilderness still glows like a fire in my soul.

Solace in Solitude

How do I keep this fire going? By permitting myself to return—repeatedly—to the memory of this solace. Recreating this time of solitude feels like a distant dream at this juncture in my life. Yet, the tapestry of neuronal connections that knows this solace in solitude allows me to touch in and revisit the experience. It's like touching my toes to the ocean's edge and having the rush of being immersed in the water return to my somatic memory. When we create mini-vacations of guided imagery based upon familiar experiences, our healing and restoration during these moments of renewal go deeper.

Utilizing our imagination and tapping into the awareness of what we are experiencing deepens our ability to integrate and live fully in the moment. For example, after the rush of a busy morning, I was hanging up wet swimming lesson items. As they began to drip, it reminded me of being in a cabin with the cool, moist forest air filtering in through the window and the delicate drip, drip, drip of the rain just beginning. The precipitation slowly falling through the branches came to mind. I imagined myself tucked into a window seat, writing, sipping tea, and watching. I was watching the words flow from my soul and onto the paper. Am I there in the woods, or am I here at my computer typing these words?

When the barriers between time and space fall away, and we are in the flow of a creative life, the importance of our true physical location becomes insignificant because we can transport our mind and our soul to that place of refuge. This connection with a place of sanctuary has been a critical piece of my mental health during the global pandemic. Visiting the places that have brought joy, rest, and rejuvenation has carried me through the moments of uncertainty. My body has not gone to these destinations, but my mind and my heart have traveled. Thinking back to our conversation about virtual reality, we see the power of this modality for pain relief. Pain is a universal experience—whether that pain is physical, emotional, or spiritual—and knowing how to cope and move through the discomfort is important to our growth. Likewise, when we see the virtual reality of life itself, we can be free from the torment of dissatisfaction with daily life.

The comfort of being alone with ourselves comes when we have found an acceptance of who we are and live in the profound joy of being our first love. Solitude is not easy for many, so be gentle with yourself as you find your path into this space. It may feel like you are traveling to an unknown universe, and you are uncertain what it will hold. Fortunately, many travelers have gone before you. The return and reintegration process of their travels brings a depth and gratitude for life that they were unacquainted with prior to their journey. You can also experience this deep connection to the unknown territories within yourself and emerge with a new reverence for life.

One way to cultivate the solace of solitude is to create a place of sanctuary within your home. Jessi Bloom shares in the opening of her book, *Creating Sanctuary*: "We all need sanctuary. We need a place where we can feel safe, one that rejuvenates us, somewhere we feel nourished and loved" (Bloom 2018, 9). Whether it's a backyard garden or a cozy spot in your dwelling space, carving out areas that help you physically rejuvenate contributes to your emotional healing. What space can you cultivate where you'll feel nourished and loved?

Currently, retreating away from home has not been an option for me, and I realize it may not be for you either. This restriction makes our need to create sanctuary in our current space even more important. To create a sensation similar to heading off to a retreat center, we may need to develop alternative ways to step away from our busy lives. How do we create a heartfelt moment where we can be alone, take a deep breath, and feel rejuvenated? Start by connecting with the awakening of your senses. Is it a walk outside with the gentle, sweet song of the birds tickling your eardrums? Maybe it's the touch of the warm sun on your skin. Or it could be the comfort of a cozy blanket while meditating in the silence of the dawn or dusk.

Whatever it is, taking time for yourself is vital for your health. So as you wandered the pages in this book, I hope you gained insight into methods of caring for and loving yourself. For in that self-care, you generate the garden of your life. And in that garden, you can plant your seeds of potentiality. So what is your garden looking like today? And what steps will you take to cultivate the garden of your dreams? The seeds within you are waiting. They are ready to burst through their coverings and unfurl into the life you want to live.

Honoring our Wholeness

One of the first foods I ate after completing my fast was an apple. I inspected the fruit with greater reverence than before, recognizing the beauty and potential it held. Next, I cut the apple into pieces and ate one. Is the apple still whole? I considered the outside and the inside, and my thoughts landed on the seeds inside. A seed is whole; it has everything it needs to become what it is destined for in its existence. The seeds hold the potential to produce another apple.

In the same way, you are whole and can live life to its fullest potential. Wholeness is not perfection. To grasp the beauty of our wholeness, we step into the innate creativity of life and see that everything needed to be whole is present. This totality is found in nature, and it's available in our lives. We are innately full and complete.

Whole, capable, and resourceful are ways most of us want to feel as we navigate life. What is whole? It's all of you, your totality. All your aspects—the things you love and find challenging about yourself—make up your personhood. What does it look like to allow yourself to be fully you? Many of us hide our talents and abilities for fear of not being accepted or being too much for others. Or we develop habits to soothe the pain. Instead of worrying about the outside world, what if you recognized that the solution lived in you? What if you loved yourself enough to attend to the part of you that is hurting? This self-love would be you living your wholeness. Give yourself permission to tend to your needs.

How do you identify your needs? Identify where things are breaking down. In this book, we explored the interrelated systems of your body and how they are orchestrated by a complex system of hormones, neurons, and signals. The systems do not operate independently. Your heart needs your lungs to oxygenate the blood. The nervous system needs muscles to make you move. There is an interconnectedness between systems. These connections tie the pieces together. Is there a weak point in one of your systems? Does your immunity need bolstering? Do you need more hydration? Return to the metaphor of the garden and consider how to cultivate health. If things are running smoothly physically, maybe your mental or spiritual health needs tending.

Our mental state is a series of connections as well. Sometimes our thoughts can dismantle these connections and tear us into pieces. Did you know that it is easier for our brain to think negative thoughts than positive ones? This thought pattern is called negativity bias. Our brains have evolved to protect us, and being more clued into the threats and dangers keeps us safe. We tend to hold on to criticisms more tightly than compliments because we avoid making the same "mistake." Life's traumas leave deeper impressions than the triumphs, and we tend to ruminate more on negative thoughts than positive ones. How do we shift our focus?

Step outside the mental constructs and see the larger fabric that makes the universe into the mysterious entity that holds time and space. This critical moment is where tapping into our spiritual health can bolster our emotional well-being. Since we pay more attention to the bad things that happen and tend to believe our thoughts are reality, things can look bleak. This cloudy perspective causes us to live in a state of confusion rather than clarity. However, when we widen our horizons, our hearts and minds expand and open our new possibilities. If we pivot the negativity as an opportunity to learn and move on, we can strengthen our resilience. We can celebrate the "mistakes" and heal from the traumas we experience in life. Our capacity is impressive, and when we recognize our ability to overcome and move beyond, we have tapped into the wholeness that is a part of our humanity.

The connections in our life bring wholeness. But, as the pandemic has taught, being alone is not easy for humans. Although there is solace in solitude, we also need community. Consider the groups and individuals that bring joy, passion, and aliveness to your soul. Where do you feel encouraged to live out your fullness and express your authenticity? Seek out the opportunity to align with those who bolster your spirit and help you soar.

Connecting with our natural surroundings also evokes feelings of wholeness. The ecosystems of the world around us buzz and hum along with unparalleled beauty. Returning to the garden metaphor, the role and importance of bees comes to mind as I think of my backyard sanctuary. The little black and yellow striped insects hustle and bustle with excitement as each new Iceland poppy opens. Their furry legs gather the pollen as the bees drink their fill of nectar. This crucial step in their process helps pollinate other flowers. The actions of the bees influence the vibrancy of my garden and thus impact my sense of joy when taking in the stunning vision of colors and textures. Constantly being aware of the interconnections of the natural world, the food it provides, and our health opens our consciousness of the holistic system we live in.

The water cycle is another amazing system to consider when contemplating wholeness. As discussed earlier in the sunrise in the garden, all water is present—it regenerates and moves through various states. Water that was once the rain is now in the ocean. As that water in the ocean evaporates and moves across time and space, it becomes the water that rains on your rooftop. If you collected that water in a gray water system, it could become the water that washes your clothes. The cycle continues. When we contemplate these vast systems that hold deep significance for our survival, we see the connections. The interdependence between humanity and our earth is indisputable.

Your life cycles—the physical, emotional, and spiritual dimensions—are ever-evolving, just as the cycles of the seasons continue as we spin on this globe through space. One path or aspect may feel out of sync, but if you see the whole picture, you may see the continual process of healing that is occurring to sustain your wholeness. The winters of our lives will bloom with the promise of spring, and the harvest of summer will compost with the leaves of fall. This process of regeneration is inherent to our humanity. From the cells of our bodies working to sustain our lives to the renewal of our thoughts, we are regenerative. There is a continual transformation in our physical, emotional, and spiritual realms. Not only do the wounds of our tissues heal, the wounds of our souls, the damaged spirit, can find restoration.

Feel the support of the systems that sustain you. There is a sphere of life-giving resources that extends from your core to the outer reaches of the universe. Zoom out and take a macroscopic look at the earth and see that we are each a microcosmic part of the whole. Not an insignificant part. A part, and all the pieces, including you, make up the whole.

Harmony

Harmony can transport us just as a well-arranged piece of music can shift our mood. I am listening to music as I write this to you. I have found that music blocks doubt and mind chatter and motivates me. I put on music to do the dishes, relax, and unwind—or carry me down the road on a long trip. This resonance is the flowing current of our lives. It is a peace that creates a timelessness that opens doors and separates the layers that are often compressed by the pressures of life. What if the harmony of our life was the music we lived to every day?

There is a congruence when the various aspects of life align. In a world where everything can feel out of sort, having an inner accord brings contentment. There may be dishes in the sink, unanswered emails, and piles of unfinished business stacking up at home and work, yet the peace that comes with living and accepting life just as it is can be profound. Too often, we think that we must have it all together and know all the answers to succeed in life. I hope your journey through this book helped you see that those thoughts are not true. Perfection is not necessary for a fulfilling life. Your beauty and wholeness as an individual are present in all stages of your personal growth life cycle and in all circumstances.

When I am in resonance with my true self, the light of the universe shines through. This brilliance comes with authenticity, awareness, and acceptance. The rhythms of nature understand this so well. Think of the flowers. They wake to the sun, they open, and they allow their full potential to radiate in absolute glory. The flowers do not hold back. Neither should we. Hear the music of your potential, connect with your creative flow, cultivate a lifestyle that supports your calling, and celebrate the beauty and mystery of life's unfolding.

There are times where harmony feels far from possible in the current time of writing this book. Unprecedented discord has taken place, and humanity is fighting to find a new path amid a global pandemic. Harmony comes when there is accord, peace, collaboration, and agreement. We are far from this balance in our current political and communal environment. The world is calling for a significant healing, and we can each respond to that beacon. But are we willing to go into the unknown? How we can participate in this healing may feel uncertain.

But as we've learned, allowing uncertainty can transport us to new destinations. The shift comes from within. We can grow our resilience and attend to our healing. When we heal, others heal. The rings of congruence echo out from our shift. The healing ripples out to others and becomes the communal healing balm that we all need. In the way of Gandhi, Mother Teresa, and individuals of influence in our world today, we can be the change. The healing flows outward from our healing, and we realize our collective wholeness.

Constantly connecting to harmony will provide guidance as you assimilate the lessons and insights of life's unfolding. In my life today, harmony is the sun shining and the brisk air after a fierce storm has quieted. These storms may be a moment in your day or years of your life. When the intensity has passed and the sweet bliss of a new day dawns, we are reminded of the harmony that hums in our lives. It may be hard to hear when the winds are howling, and the rain and hail are pounding on the windows of our soul. When the noise is deafening, we can retreat and connect with our authentic self. Know that storms do pass, and the bliss of a new day, a new moment in time, is enough to connect us with the harmony needed to bring our seeds of potentiality to a harvest of insight.

Harvest of Insight Meditation

You are standing at the threshold of your inner terrain. The sun is rising, and the faint glow turns into a flood of brilliant light illuminating all that you have brought to this moment.
You see the valleys you have traveled and the mountain peaks you have climbed.
Standing at the edge of your view, you stretch out your arms and take flight, gliding over the grandmother tree. You see her roots reaching deep into the earth and drinking from the waters of the babbling brook. The wind catches your wings, and the flowing current reminds you of the flow you find when connecting with your creativity.
You do not know where you are heading. The uncertainty is liberating and frees you to hear the faint melodies calling you into the dance of synchronicity. You feel alive and connected. Your passions are aligned with your actions.
In your vibrance, you shed your fears, you let go, and you arrive at the clearing. As your feet touch the cool, moist soil, you feel nourished. Roots grow from the soles of your feet and push through the earth below. You are growing and connecting with the earth that holds you. As you are fed from below, your spine lengthens, your breath deepens, and your arms reach up into the sky. You are emerging.
Then you feel the sweet presence of the sunlight gently warming your skin. Your heart opens like a rose unfurling its petals. You stand in awe. The garden you have planted from your seeds of potentiality has bloomed into full abundance. Love and joy fill your entire being.
You recognize your wholeness.
Here in the quiet moment of your joyful bliss, you find solace in the stillness. Everything slows, and you can see the absolute

harmony of your life. This radiance is the garden that grows within. It is overflowing with life. Your life. It is your harvest. A harvest of insight that has come from your journey of creating, cultivating, and celebrating.

May the glow of your insight bless you and provide the light to guide you.

appendix a

THOUGHTS ON SEEDS

Resource Section on Seeds and Soil Advocacy

Written by Rachel Parent
From: www.seewhatgrows.org/every-seed-story/

"The act of exchanging seeds allowed people to exchange knowledge, culture, and history. Globally in the past 80 years we've lost over 93% of our seed variety in food production. There are currently over 80,000 edible plants varieties, yet only 150 types are being harvested, and only 8 are being traded globally.

If all of our resources were used properly it would be possible to increase biodiversity, food distribution, decrease hunger, improve soil health, and provide opportunity and freedom to farmers.

Seeds hold a special importance to people, especially within indigenous cultures, as the seeds represent the hardships, the struggle, and the perseverance to maintain the land and its peoples. Traditionally, the selection, preservation, and fundamental knowledge and practice of passing on and exchanging seeds has been the main duties of women. Historically, seed preservation was a fundamental rule for the survival of humanity.

Seeds, in all reality, are as diverse as we are. They're filled with life, each holding their own intelligence, uniqueness, and potential. They come in all shapes and sizes, from a tiny speck to a giant seed, such as the avocado. They have different colors and textures. Some are protected by the outer layer of a fruit. Others have to be submerged in water for long periods of time to germinate. Some float through the air, while others travel great distances on the fur of animals. Some even have to go through the digestive system of certain species before they can germinate. Most amazingly, the tiny seed that grows into the Giant Sequoia can only grow after a forest fire."

Rachel Parent is a guest blog writer for See What Grows and founder of the nonprofit organization Kids Right to Know.

KidsRightToKnow.org
Gen-Earth.Org

Other seed sources to check out:

https://trueloveseeds.com/blogs/satpradio
https://stories.kitchenaid.com/article/preserving-culture-through-seeds
https://kisstheground.com/advocacy/
https://seewhatgrows.org/

Appendix B

NOTES OF HOPE

By David Villareal
www.thetherapeuticguitarist.com

I was blessed to have been born into a musical family. My father, who was a self-taught musician, was my greatest inspiration. He shared his passion for music with my sister and me, starting when we were young. My father was very involved in providing music for religious services and mentored me in that ministry. In addition to regular church services, the religious community often asked us to provide music to nursing home facilities, prisons, and small community functions. These experiences laid the foundation for what would become my call to service.

As time went on, I continued to assist in religious services when possible but ventured out onto other musical paths. I played in dance bands, performed for children, provided music for flamenco, and played guitar at the bedside of family members who were ill.

Little did I realize how much of an impact these experiences would have on me and others throughout my life. I found that music was like a jewel with many facets available to explore. I studied guitar for years and often wondered why I was doing this other than for personal fulfillment. I had the passion for learning but no real goal in mind. But eventually, purpose found me—I came to realize that I had reached the pinnacle of my journey and understood the path that was laid out for me.

My true calling was revealed to me when my young daughter-in-law, Becca, was diagnosed with cancer. While in the hospital, I spent many hours playing for her. One day, a lady came in with a harp and asked Becca if she would like to hear some calming music. I was absolutely mesmerized by the session. She noticed my guitar case, and we ended up having a wonderful conversation about her work at the hospital. She mentioned that they were looking for another musician, specifically a guitarist, and asked that I consider joining. I didn't hesitate to say yes because I genuinely felt called and knew in my heart that I needed to be part of this community.

The only requirement was that I participate in an accredited program in clinical music. Throughout the course, I learned that this was not just about playing music, but it was also about gaining a scientific knowledge of sound and how it aids the healing process.

Stop and say the word "sound" and think about it. What do you hear? What comes to mind? Is it something pleasant? Something annoying? Sound is a vibration. We not only *hear* sound, but we can *feel* it as well. Just as we can feel the vibrations of a large truck as it passes by, our body feels the vibrations of music. Sound penetrates and has physiological effects on us, affecting our blood pressure, heart, and respiration rates. Our physical response is rooted in the brain. We are born with the ability to respond to music both physically and emotionally. Our hearing is one of the first senses that comes into play and one of the last to leave us. Studies have shown that we are able to hear in our mother's womb just as we have the ability to hear underwater. It is also the sense that continues working even if we're unconscious. It's measurable. I can play music at the bedside to a patient in a coma, watch the monitor for blood pressure, pulse, and respiration, and actually *see* the changes when music is present. It's fascinating to observe the profound calming effect music has on humans and animals. I enjoy the challenge of the frenetic energy found in the emergency room. I close my eyes, start by playing slowly, quietly, and arrhythmically, and calmness can be felt within 15 to 20 minutes. A similar calming response happens with an agitated patient or patients with mental illness. Music is powerful!!

Another aspect to note is silence. Silence has a relationship with sound. Our brains have the capabilities to fill in notes when the main note is intentionally silent. Silence is very important in the listening as it allows the brain to decode musical structure. I think it's akin to watering a potted plant. It's natural to water the plant and stop for a moment to allow it to soak in before adding more. In therapeutic music, long pauses or intentional silence add to the effectiveness of the session. Claude Debussy stated that the music is the silence between the notes, and I think he was onto something.

Lastly, the role of the live musician is presence, emotion, and intent. Since music is created by humans, I feel it's fair to say that it's created from emotion, and when shared, it can elicit emotion. Music is the emotion of the composer translated into sound. It has the ability to allow us to feel and recall moments in time and maybe manipulate our emotions. As a clinical musician, my intent is to be a calming presence. My hope is to emit the emotions of love and caring to each individual through music. I know my calling is to be present in the intimate setting of sick or dying individuals and their families. There is a need to honor the significance of each person. Each person is a human life, a human spirit. Despite social, educational, or financial status, we are all significant and require the same basic needs. Personally, music is more than a song; it's my passion and purpose.

References

Allen, Jennifer. 2009. *Bone Knowing: A True Story of Coming to Life in the Face of Impending Loss.* United States: Jujupress.

Andreae, Laura C. 2018. "Adult Neurogenesis in Humans: Dogma Overturned, Again and Again?" *Science Translational Medicine* 10 (436): eaat3893. https://doi.org/10.1126/scitranslmed.aat3893.

Arrien, Angeles. 2013. *Living in Gratitude: Mastering the Art of Giving Thanks Every Day: A Month-by-Month Guide.* Boulder, CO: Sounds True, Inc.

Begley, Sharon. 2007. *Train Your Mind, Change Your Brain: How a New Science Reveals Our Extraordinary Potential to Transform Ourselves.* New York: Ballantine Books.

Bloom, Jessi. 2018. *Creating Sanctuary: Sacred Garden Spaces, Plant-Based Medicine, and Daily Practices to Achieve Happiness and Well-Being.* Portland, OR: Timber Press.

Brittain, Christina. 2016. *The Lighten Your Vibe Coloring Book.* Bloomington, IN: Balboa Press.

Campbell, Joseph, Bill D. Moyers, and Betty S. Flowers. 1991. *The Power of Myth.* New York: Anchor Books.

Carver, Courtney. 2017. *Soulful Simplicity: How Living with Less Can Lead to so Much More.* New York: Tarcher Perigee.

Csikszentmihalyi, Mihaly. 2009. *Flow: The Psychology of Optimal Experience.* Harper Perennial Modern Classics. New York: HarperPerennial.

Csikszentmihalyi, Mihaly. 2013. *Creativity: The Psychology of Discovery and Invention.* First Harper Perennial Modern Classics edition. New York: Harper Perennial Modern Classics.

DiGiacomo, Liscia. 2021. "Life as a Somatic Exploration." *Dancing Hands Bodywork* (blog). May 24, 2021. https://dancinghands-bodywork.com/new-blog-1/2021/5/21/3093fi4pkdx0w422k9f8wkkt6y5r5r.

Dweck, Carol S. 2008. *Mindset: The New Psychology of Success.* New York: Ballantine Books.

Emoto, Masaru, and David A. Thayne. 2011. *The Secret Life of Water.* New York: Atria Books.

Gold, Aviva, and Elena Oumano. 1998. *Painting from the Source: Awakening Your Artist's Soul in Everyone.* New York: HarperPerennial.

Gold, Joshua, and Joseph Ciorciari. 2020. "A Review on the Role of the Neuroscience of Flow States in the Modern World." *Behavioral Sciences* 10 (9): 137. https://doi.org/10.3390/bs10090137.

Gupta, Anita, Kevin Scott, and Matthew Dukewich. 2017. "Innovative Technology Using Virtual Reality in the Treatment of Pain: Does It Reduce Pain via Distraction, or Is There More to It?" *Pain Medicine* 19 (1): 151–59. https://doi.org/10.1093/pm/pnx109.

Hari Dass. 2000. *Everyday Peace: Letters for Life.* Santa Cruz, CA: Sri Rama Publishing.

Heatherton, Todd F. 2011. "Neuroscience of Self and Self-Regulation." *Annual Review of Psychology* 62 (1): 363–390. https://doi.org/10.1146/annurev.psych.121208.131616.

Hebb, Donald O. 1974. *The Organization of Behavior: A Neuropsychological Theory*. New York: Wiley.

Institute of Medicine (US) Committee on Quality of Health Care in America. 2000. *To Err Is Human: Building a Safer Health System*. Edited by Linda T. Kohn, Janet M. Corrigan, and Molla S. Donaldson. Washington, DC: National Academies Press. http://www.ncbi.nlm.nih.gov/books/NBK225182/.

International Expressive Arts Therapy Association. n.d. "About Us." Accessed July 23, 2021. https://www.ieata.org/.

Johnson, Amy. 2016. *The Little Book of Big Change: The No-Willpower Approach to Breaking Any Habit*. Oakland, CA: New Harbinger Publications, Inc.

Jung, C. G., and Sonu Shamdasani. 2010. *Synchronicity: An Acausal Connecting Principle*. Translated by Richard F. C. Hull. Princeton, NJ: Princeton University Press.

Kiss the Ground. n.d. "Stewardship Education." Accessed September 13, 2021. https://kisstheground.com/stewardship/.

Kondo, Marie. 2014. *The Life-Changing Magic of Tidying Up: The Japanese Art of Decluttering and Organizing*. Translated by Cathy Hirano. Berkeley, CA: Ten Speed Press.

Macaulay, David. 1988. *The Way Things Work*. New York: Houghton Mifflin.

Murray, Elizabeth. 2014. *Living Life in Full Bloom: 120 Daily Practices to Deepen Your Passion, Creativity & Relationships*. New York: Rodale.

Ober, Clinton, Stephen T. Sinatra, and Martin Zucker. 2014. *Earthing: The Most Important Health Discovery Ever!* Laguna Beach, CA: Basic Health Publications, Inc.

Plotkin, Bill. 2003. *Soulcraft: Crossing into the Mysteries of Nature and Psyche*. Novato, CA: New World Library.

Plotkin, Bill. n.d. A Talk with Bill Plotkin about *Wild Mind.* Accessed August 1, 2021. https://www.newworldlibrary.com/Default.aspx?tabid=63&AuthorID=1647#.YVFRg7hKhPY.

Roth, Gabrielle, and John Loudon. 1998. *Maps to Ecstasy: A Healing Journey for the Untamed Spirit.* Revised edition. Novato, Calif: New World Library.

Ryan, Ashley. 2016. "Coloring Books and Creativity." *Newport Beach Magazine*, May 2016. https://expressiveartstraining.com/articles/

Shatz, Carla J. 1992. "The Developing Brain." *Scientific American* 267 (3): 60–67.

Shiva, Vandana. 2014. *Sacred Seed.* Point Reyes, CA: The Golden Sufi Center.

Singer, Michael A. 2013. *The Untethered Soul: The Journey Beyond Yourself.* Oakland, CA: New Harbinger Publications, Inc.

Singer, Michael A. 2015. *The Surrender Experiment: My Journey into Life's Perfection.* First edition. New York: Harmony Books.

Sorin, Fran. 2004. *Digging Deep: Unearthing Your Creative Roots through Gardening.* New York: Warner Books.

Stevens, Christine. 2003. *The Art and Heart of Drum Circles.* First Edition. Milwaukee, WI: Hal Leonard Corporation.

Wager, Tor D., James K. Rilling, Edward E. Smith, Alex Sokolik, Kenneth L. Casey, Richard J. Davidson, Stephen M. Kosslyn, Robert M. Rose, and Jonathan D. Cohen. 2004. "Placebo-Induced Changes in fMRI in the Anticipation and Experience of Pain." *Science* 303 (5661): 1162–67. https://doi.org/10.1126/science.1093065.

Resources

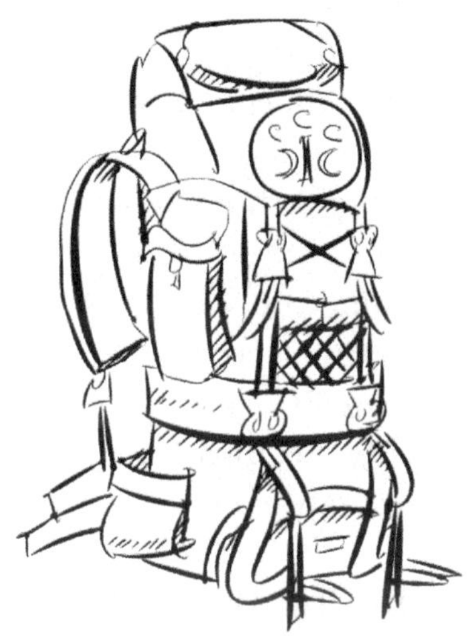

Gifts of the Grandmother Tree (Chapter 1)

- Cristin DeVine and Peter Fonken
    - http://www.counselingcarmel.com/
- Bill Plotkin and Animus Valley Institute:
    - https://www.animas.org/
- South Park Yoga (formerly Ginseng Yoga)
    - https://southpark.yoga/
- Laura Plumb
    - https://lauraplumb.com/
- Jane Goldberg
    - https://expressiveartstraining.com/
- Esalen Institute
    - https://www.esalen.org/

- Mount Madonna Center
    - o https://www.mountmadonna.org/
- Joseph Campbell
    - o Campbell, Joseph. 2008. *The Hero with a Thousand Faces.* Third edition. Bollingen Series XVII. Novato, CA: New World Library.
    - o https://www.jcf.org/
- Sharon Begley
    - o http://www.sharonlbegley.com/
- Deepak Chopra
    - o https://www.deepakchopra.com/
- Jon Kabat-Zinn
    - o https://www.mindfulnesscds.com/
    - o https://www.youtube.com/watch?v=JQgkGBdt89A
- Mindfulness Research Collaborative (MRC)
    - o https://davidvago.bwh.harvard.edu/mindfulness-research-collaborative-mrc/

Musings of the Babbling Brook (Chapter2)

- Amy Johnson
    - o https://dramyjohnson.com/
- Michael Singer
    - o https://untetheredsoul.com/
- Jennifer Allen
    - o https://boneknowing.com/
    - o https://anchor.fm/boneknowing

Arrivals of the Flowing Current (Chapter 3)

- For more on Flow:
    - o https://www.increasemyefficiency.com/flow/
    - o https://www.deanbokhari.com/flow/
    - o https://www.psychologytoday.com/us/articles/199707/finding-flow

- Aviva Gold and Painting from the Source
  - o https://paintingfromthesource.com/

Productions of the Dance of Synchronicity (Chapter 4)

- NIA Technique
  - o https://nianow.com/
- Shakti Rising
  - o https://www.shaktirising.org/
- Dunn High School
  - o https://www.dunnschool.org/
- David Villareal
  - o https://thetherapeuticguitarist.com/home
- Gabrielle Roth and 5Rythms Dance
  - o https://www.5rhythms.com/

Sacraments of the Clearing (Chapter 5)

- Courtney Carver's website and community: Be More with Less
  - o https://bemorewithless.com/
- Vipassana meditation retreats
  - o https://www.dhamma.org/en-US/index
- Christina Brittain
  - o https://christinabrittain.com/
- IEATA: International Expressive Arts Therapy Association
  - o https://www.ieata.org/

Discoveries from the Turning of the Soil (Chapter 6)

- Gratitude resources:
  - o https://gratefulness.org/
  - o https://ggsc.berkeley.edu/
- Dancing Hands Massage Therapy—Liscia DiGiacomo
  - o https://dancinghandsbodywork.com/

Explorations for the Roots Push Through (Chapter 7)

- Great Articles:
  - o https://thriveglobal.com/stories/how-to-let-go-of-your-expectations-and-live-a-happier-life/
  - o https://organizationalhabits.com/2017/03/19/mapping-your-personal-ecosystem/
  - o https://depthnotwidth.com/living-life-on-purpose-your-personal-mission-statement/

Inspirations for the Joy of Abundance (Chapter 9)

- Mindset
  - o https://profiles.stanford.edu/carol-dweck
  - o https://www.mindsetworks.com/science/
  - o https://www.mindsetkit.org/

Fruits of the Harvest of Insight (Chapter 10)

- Jessi Bloom
  - o https://www.nwbloom.com/company/the-team/
- Books on Sacred Space:
  - o *Cultivating Sacred Space: Gardening for the Soul* by Elizabeth Murray
  - o *Sacred Ceremony: How to Create Ceremonies for Healing, Transitions, and Celebrations* by Steven D. Farmer
  - o *The Art of Ritual: Creating and Performing Ceremonies for Growth and Change* by Renee Beck
  - o *The Garden Awakening* by Mary Reynolds

Meaningful Meditations

Recordings of the meditations found at the end of each chapter are read by and set to the original healing music of Farmer Dave (http://farmerdavescher.com/). They are available for your listening enjoyment on the book website: www.seedsofpotentiality.com

Acknowledgments

This book would not have been feasible without the love, support, and guidance of my father. His dedication to the art of writing was evident in his interest in developing the seed thoughts that grew and bloomed on the pages of this book. I want to thank him for the endless hours he spent reading and rereading the words that started as seeds and eventually became the story you now hold. His support would not have been possible without the additional love and nurturance of my mother, who encouraged me to pursue this dream and to reach for the stars. I am deeply blessed to have amazing parents who have tended to my life and helped me grow my seeds of potentiality.

My dear husband, Brendan, is the artist who took my sketches and concepts and brought them to life as digital art. His patience and support made writing this book possible. From watching Declan to reading and providing feedback, his strength of consistently caring meant volumes to me.

My sweet Declan provided inspiration and ideas that evolved with a spiritual synchronicity as I wrote the book. His interest in looking deeper and asking "why?" pushed me in my own desire to reach further. He has shown me that we truly are made of stardust, and the concepts that appear imaginary may be more of a reality than I might have originally thought possible.

The core of my personal story shared in this book is based on the life-changing vision fast I was guided on by my dear friends Cristin and Peter. The hours they spent preparing, leading, and supporting those of us who ventured on the pilgrimage provided the foundation for meaningful change and evolution. I am deeply thankful for their lives and how they tirelessly give back to their community and Mother Earth.

As I connect with the individuals whose threads have been woven into the tapestry of my life experience shared in this book, I am aware of the value that connections and community play in our lives. I honor the generations of spiritual leaders who have been at the core of communities like Esalen Institute and Mount Madonna Center. My time in these places planted seeds that have grown into attributes of my life that will stay with me to the end.

The individuals who have tended to the cultivation of these seeds have been mentioned throughout my writing, and if you would like to learn more about their lives and services, you can find more information in the resources section. Their books, services, recipes, paintings, and presence are a gift to this world. One individual I would like to pay tribute to is Sharon Begley, a science writer who passed away while I was writing the book. Her writing inspired and challenged me to dig deep and look at the science behind what I wanted to communicate in my book. I was drawn to reach out to her, and that is when I learned of her death. I am inspired by women who look for answers and seek out understanding. I was touched by this reflection in the following article:

In the hours after Sharon died on Saturday at 64, due to complications of the cancer, her longtime friend and colleague Melinda Beck was unsure of what to do with herself and opened their college yearbook. "In her little entry, she wrote that she hoped to be a science journalist," Beck said, a little after midnight.

"What an understatement. It's kind of like Louis Pasteur saying, 'Gee, I'd like to be a biologist.'" (https://www.statnews.com/2021/01/17/sharon-begley-path-breaking-science-journalist-dies/)

Sharon lived out her seeds of potentiality and strove to share what she learned with the world. I wanted to take a moment to honor her here and thank her for the amazing journalism she brought to the world.

In conclusion, I would like to thank Jared Rosen for his gift of bringing books to life. His guidance and creativity helped open the conduit that poured my life experience onto the pages. Joyce Walker and Vicki Ronaldson were the empathic and supportive editors who helped shape and transform the original manuscript into the final product you hold today. I am thankful for DreamSculpt and their vision to support new authors like myself. Their partnership with Waterside Productions has provided the framework to take the concepts within me and develop an ecosystem for sharing them with others.

About the Author

Dr. Melissa Thompson is a lifelong learner who takes each experience and weaves it into the tapestry of insight and collective wisdom that guides her on her life's journey. Her dedication to understanding the world around her—from the microcosm of how pharmacological substances work in our bodies to the macrocosm of humanity's interchange with the earth—leads her to seek out a deeper level of knowing. From pharmacy school to transpersonal psychology, Melissa has studied the layers of mind, body, and spirit. Diving into the studies of yoga, mindfulness, integrative medicine, expressive arts, and more, she expands her awareness. Beyond the classroom, Melissa takes her daily life experiences as a mother, daughter, and wife and reflects on the significance of these relationships. Open to constantly learning more, she hopes to continually create, cultivate, and celebrate the garden of her life.

Contact Information

Melissa Thompson, PharmD, MA
melissa@seedsofpotentiality.com
www.seedsofpotentiality.com
www.createcultivatecelebrate.com

Made in the USA
Las Vegas, NV
17 December 2021